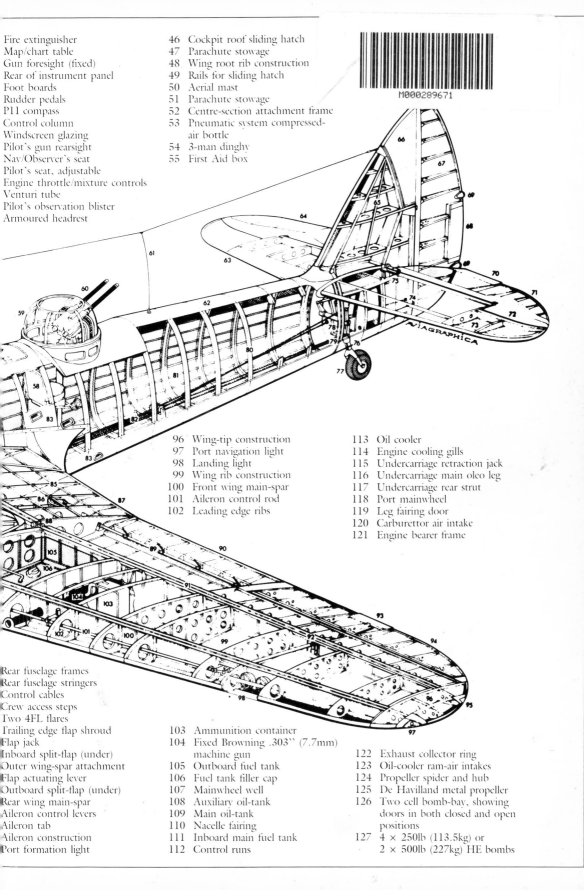

Fire extinguisher
Map/chart table
Gun foresight (fixed)
Rear of instrument panel
Foot boards
Rudder pedals
P11 compass
Control column
Windscreen glazing
Pilot's gun rearsight
Nav/Observer's seat
Pilot's seat, adjustable
Engine throttle/mixture controls
Venturi tube
Pilot's observation blister
Armoured headrest

46 Cockpit roof sliding hatch
47 Parachute stowage
48 Wing root rib construction
49 Rails for sliding hatch
50 Aerial mast
51 Parachute stowage
52 Centre-section attachment frame
53 Pneumatic system compressed-
     air bottle
54 3-man dinghy
55 First Aid box

96 Wing-tip construction
97 Port navigation light
98 Landing light
99 Wing rib construction
100 Front wing main-spar
101 Aileron control rod
102 Leading edge ribs

113 Oil cooler
114 Engine cooling gills
115 Undercarriage retraction jack
116 Undercarriage main oleo leg
117 Undercarriage rear strut
118 Port mainwheel
119 Leg fairing door
120 Carburettor air intake
121 Engine bearer frame

Rear fuselage frames
Rear fuselage stringers
Control cables
Crew access steps
Two 4FL flares
Trailing edge flap shroud
Flap jack
Inboard split-flap (under)
Outer wing-spar attachment
Flap actuating lever
Outboard split-flap (under)
Rear wing main-spar
Aileron control levers
Aileron tab
Aileron construction
Port formation light

103 Ammunition container
104 Fixed Browning .303" (7.7mm)
     machine gun
105 Outboard fuel tank
106 Fuel tank filler cap
107 Mainwheel well
108 Auxiliary oil-tank
109 Main oil-tank
110 Nacelle fairing
111 Inboard main fuel tank
112 Control runs

122 Exhaust collector ring
123 Oil-cooler ram-air intakes
124 Propeller spider and hub
125 De Havilland metal propeller
126 Two cell bomb-bay, showing
     doors in both closed and open
     positions
127 4 × 250lb (113.5kg) or
     2 × 500lb (227kg) HE bombs

Patrick Stephens Limited, a member of the Haynes Publishing Group, has published authoritative, quality books for enthusiasts for more than 20 years. During that time the company has established a reputation as one of the world's leading publishers of books on aviation, maritime, military, model-making, motor cycling, motoring, motor racing, railway and railway modelling subjects. Readers or authors with suggestions for books they would like to see published are invited to write to: The Editorial Director, Patrick Stephens Limited, Sparkford, Nr Yeovil, Somerset BA22 7JJ.

The Forgotten Bomber

The story of the restoration of the world's
only airworthy Bristol Blenheim

Graham Warner

Patrick Stephens Limited

First published in 1991

British Library Cataloguing in Publication Data

Warner, Graham
    The forgotten bomber: the story of the restoration of the world's only airworthy
    Bristol Blenheim.
    1. Great Britain. Royal Air Force. Bomber aeroplanes, history.
    I. Title
    623.74630941

ISBN 1-85260-307-0

Patrick Stephens Limited is a member of the Haynes Publishing Group P.L.C.,
Sparkford, Nr Yeovil, Somerset, BA22 7JJ.

Printed in Great Britain by J.H. Haynes & Co Ltd.

10 9 8 7 6 5 4 3 2 1

Contents

Acknowledgements

I should like to thank the members of the team who have answered my questions so patiently, explained to me some of the more technical operations involved in the restoration process, and reminded me of some aspects or difficulties that I had overlooked, so that I could describe them all — in layman's language — more adequately and understandably when compiling this book.

Acknowledgements and thanks for the many interesting and fascinating photographs are due mainly to John 'Smudger' Smith who has supplied by far the largest number, for as you will see he kept an excellent and detailed photographic record of the restoration while it was underway. The most informative Blenheim cut-away drawing by Aviagraphica for Pilot Press, that forms the endpapers, is produced by kind permission of Greenborough Associates and appeared in *Air Enthusiast* issue No 28 of July 1985.

Other photographs were kindly supplied by Clive Norman, Mike Shreeve, Chris Burkett, Colin and David Swann, John Dibbs and Patrick Bunce. I regret that in the case of some of the very early illustrations I am unable to attribute the source. I hope the photographers, both those mentioned and those I am prevented from mentioning, will forgive me for not crediting their illustrations individually, for they have all made a notable contribution to the interest of this book.

Most sincere thanks too are due to Lord Rothermere for maintaining his keen family interest in the Blenheim. His kind and supportive attitude to both the initial and current Blenheim restorations has been a great inspiration to the whole Blenheim team. This active encouragement and practical assistance from such a distinguished and busy man, particularly in the support he gave to the limited edition Blenheim prints — which certainly assured their success — has been absolutely invaluable and is much appreciated.

As mentioned in the text, Richard Lucraft has been of enormous help too. The contributions to The Blenheim Appeal from the two special limited edition prints mentioned above — conceived, arranged and marketed with great flair and skill by Richard and his small organization — were by far the most significant received. In fact they contributed about half of the total receipts of the fund, so mere thanks seem entirely inadequate. Without Richard's great efforts for the appeal we would not be nearly as advanced as we are with the second restoration.

Most heartfelt thanks are given to each and every person who has sent a donation to The Blenheim Appeal however large or small. In many instances the contributions were from pensioners and clearly not easily spared, so their unstinted generosity is all the more remarkable; many hundreds of letters said, 'We just wish we could do more,' or words to that effect. Such moral support is just as important and encouraging to the team as direct donations. Our main problem concerning the appeal is that the financial demands on the Blenheim restoration fund are continuous over the months and years, and it is very difficult to keep an appeal of this nature in the public eye and memory over such an extended period.

I would like to thank Patrick Stephens for his personal encouragement and kind support for this reluctant first-time author; and Darryl Reach, the Editorial Director of the publishers Patrick Stephens Ltd, for his most understanding and helpful attitude.

My dear wife Shirley who not only puts up with my long absence from home when I am at Duxford, but also patiently read the draft of this book and made many helpful suggestions, I feel deserves more than just thanks. That reminds me that the wives of all the team members really must be thanked for accepting with so much tolerance and understanding the prolonged periods spent by their husbands working at Duxford. It was apposite that when we attended the Battle of Britain Air Display at RAF Abingdon last year with parts of the wrecked Blenheim, that we stayed in The Dog House — actually an excellent hotel!

With regard to the practical assistance received from companies in the aviation industry during the restoration of the Blenheim, I have tried to give the proper credit due for this in the text at the appropriate points, for the rebuild to airworthiness could not have been completed without such generous support.

Some individuals and companies merit special mention and appreciation however: Phillip Birtles and John Waymark of BAe at Hatfield and Welwyn, Bill Ball and Bill Bainbridge of BAe at Lostock, Ellis Johns of BAe at Filton; Lord King, Chairman of British Airways; Mike Longroft of Varne Engineering Ltd at Biggleswade; John Tuffin then of KeyMed Ltd; Len Murray and Albert Farmer of Morse Controls (Teleflex); Peter Paige of DAS and Duxford Displays Ltd; Keith Drummond of Trust Parts, Cambridge; J.E. Hyde of Sil-Mid Ltd; Brian Sayer of Air UK; John Dovey of Capel Plant Ltd; Brett Matthews of PPG Industries UK; and Dr R.T. von Bergen of Edgar Vaughan & Co Ltd.

Since writing these acknowledgements, it grieves me to have to record that the team have lost their Chief Pilot, John Larcombe. He did all the test flying in the first Blenheim and 'checked out' the pilots on all our other ex-military aircraft, he was an ex-RAF Qualified Flying Instructor and latterly a Training Captain with British Airways. 'Larks' — and he certainly lived up to his nickname — was held in the highest regard by all at Duxford, but especially by the Blenheim team, as he was a constant inspiration to all of us. We know of no better, safer, more gifted and conscientous pilot than John. To say that he will be missed enormously by the team seems so inadequate; his loss leaves a central void virtually impossible to fill.

He came down on 4 June 1990 in The Fighter Collection's Bell P63 'Kingcobra' soon after take-off from a French airfield where he had performed his usual immaculate display the day before. The aircraft had a major engine problem and caught fire, and although he had a parachute it is believed that he stayed in the cockpit to guide the doomed aircraft clear of a village at the cost of his own life. His selfless contribution to, and natural leadership of, the flying operations of the team were absolutely invaluable.

So he heads the list of those included in the greatest 'thank you' of all which, as I have tried to make clear throughout this book, deservedly belongs to each and every member of the Blenheim team. For it was the team themselves, so ably led by John Larcombe on the flying side and John Romain on the engineering side, who resurrected the Blenheim with their own hands. I only guided them and made the restoration possible — they did all the work.

It was their personal effort, time and dedication put into the project so unselfishly throughout the long years of painstaking restoration; the constant application of their varied skills and abilities; and their persistent ingenuity in overcoming so many problems, that made it possible for a derelict, forgotten bomber to return in triumph to the skies once more.

These same sterling qualities of dedication and unrivalled expertise displayed by the team then are again being devoted to making another decrepit Blenheim fit to fly. Without the team it would have been impossible for the restored Blenheim to have flown at all — through them a Blenheim *will* fly again!

John Larcombe

Ashdon, Essex, 1990

The present Viscount Rothermere inspecting the cockpit of the Blenheim from the pilot's seat at Biggin Hill in June 1987. The aircraft is surrounded by press photographers. This view shows the brass gun-firing button on the right of the control column 'spectacles' with the brake-lever on the left; the gunsight is in front of Lord Rothermere's head. The pilot's view over the 'scalloped' port side of the nose can be seen through the windscreen.

Foreword

by The Rt Hon The Viscount Rothermere, FRSA, FBIM, Commander of the
Order of Merit (Italy), and Order of the Lion (Finland)

I f asked which aircraft was used for the first offensive attack of the Second World War, sunk the first U-boat, bombed the German fleet assembling to invade our shores, was the first aircraft to be fitted with radar and used as a night fighter, few people would name the Blenheim bomber.

Yet the Blenheim proudly held these achievements and many more on its service record, and remained in active deployment in all the theatres of war until the cessation of fighting in the Far East in 1945.

The Blenheim bomber in its former guise as a six-seater executive aircraft had caught my grandfather's eye in 1934 when, with the hindsight of a past Secretary of State for Air, he recognised its potential as a fighting aircraft well suited, and much needed, to fill a vacuum for the Royal Air Force. He was so convinced of the merit and potential of this fine aircraft that he financed and presented the prototype to the RAF under the name 'Britain First'.

The determination to rebuild the restored Blenheim bomber after its disastrous mishap in 1987 would never have been found had it not played such a courageous and important part in the Second World War. This is illustrated by the spirit and encouragement of the survivors who are determined that a Blenheim will again fly as a tribute to the courage of the young men who died on some of the most perilous missions of the war.

This book pays tribute not only to those who flew the aircraft on active service but also to the dedication and skill of the men who, having seen twelve years of hard work so cruelly destroyed in a fraction of a minute, without hesitation took up the challenge to rebuild once more this aircraft which played such a vital but under-appreciated part in the Second World War.

The unsung hero

Why restore a 45-year-old Bristol Blenheim to make it fit to fly again? Who would even consider such a seemingly impossible undertaking? No one had attempted to do so before, had they? What was so special about the Blenheim anyway? After all, it didn't do much in the war did it?

I will try to answer these and other questions that have been asked during the course of the lengthy restoration of this almost forgotten wartime bomber; a restoration completed successfully, much to the surprise of many in the aviation world, so that it became the only flying example in the world. For example, many people have asked just how we came to choose this particular derelict hulk from the hundreds of different aircraft types decaying in scrapyards and rotting away in odd corners of deserted airfields all over the world. Did the Blenheim really deserve this unique resurrection?

We are convinced not only that it did but also that it was long overdue.

In the course of our research to ensure that our restoration was entirely accurate and authentic in every detail, we discovered just how very important this aircraft was in the history of the Royal Air Force, and how it was pressed into desperate use in a variety of roles — for many of which it was not suitable — because early in the Second World War it was the only offensive aircraft that the RAF possessed in any significant numbers.

We began to realize that our task was to rehabilitate not just an old airframe but also the very reputation of an excellent aircraft. The considerable and consistent contributions to the war effort made by Bristol Blenheims had for a long time been largely ignored. Their multifarious roles, all-round ability and immense usefulness had been seriously understated by many historians, and far from the importance of the Blenheim becoming recognized, however belatedly, the Blenheim seemed to be in danger of fading from the public memory altogether. We could see why most official historians had tended to sweep the operations of the Blenheims well under the carpet, for they were not associated with glamorous or successful events, operating during a period of the war when the Allies suffered mainly retreat or defeat. The Ministry of Information needed both glamour and success to capture the imagination of the wartime populace. The harsh reality was that, although fine aircraft and a joy to fly, from an operational viewpoint Blenheims were ill-equipped, and poorly armed and armoured. Their performance had become inadequate, and their losses were appalling.

Blenheims and their brave crews were thrown into the breach time and time again and suffered accordingly. Wartime propagandists could not make much of those unpalatable facts, so they quickly glossed over the discouraging and disturbing aspects. In 1940 they were quick to seize the opportunity to emphasize the heroic deeds of the Spitfires and Hurricanes of Fighter Command in the Battle of Britain. But the deeds of the Blenheim crews were no less heroic for being unsung.

The role of the Blenheim in deterring the German invasion of these islands in 1940 has not been properly acknowledged either. It was mainly their constant attacks by day and night on enemy shipping and transport generally, and on the invasion barges gathering in the channel ports in particular, that worried the German Navy so much that it was unable to support the proposed large-scale seaborne landing on these shores. Hitler first postponed then abandoned Operation 'Sealion' and turned his attentions eastwards. Even with the advantage of hindsight most post-war historians have failed to give the Blenheim Squadrons sufficient credit for their great efforts which contributed very significantly to this most fateful decision. For example, in the excellent *Aircraft at War* series of Ian Allan titles, there are no less than four separate volumes devoted to one already well-known British bomber — *Lancaster at War*, *One*, *Two*, *Three*, and *Four* — and even a *Lincoln at War* (which it wasn't really, apart from the Malayan emergency), but not even a single volume to cover the Blenheim, which was well and truly 'at war' all over the world!

The deeper we delved into the story of the Blenheim in RAF service the more we learnt about the incredible determination and dedication to duty of the 'Blenheim Boys', often pressing home their attacks in the face of daunting odds with an almost reckless courage. They were certainly aware of the vulnerability of their aircraft because they had seen so many of their fellows shot down, but they did not fail to give of their best and all too often they paid with their lives. We learnt also of the quite extraordinary affection that the Blenheim crews had for the aircraft itself, despite the heavy casualties they frequently suffered.

We knew that at the start of the war the RAF had more Bristol Blenheims in service than any other type of aircraft, a total of 1,089 as opposed to less than 200 each of the other main Bomber types, Vickers Wellingtons and Armstrong-Whitworth Whitleys, plus some Handley-Page Hampdens and several hundred Avro Ansons and the single-engined Fairey Battle. Although both latter types had been obsolete for some time for operational use by then, the Battles were thrown against the blitzkreig attack on France in May 1940 alongside the Blenheims, but ineffectively and with losses even worse than those suffered by the Blenheims.

We knew too that the Blenheim was the only aircraft to serve in every one of the Commands that then comprised the Royal Air Force (Bomber, Fighter, Coastal, Army Co-operation and Training Commands), and in every Theatre of War. We did not know that no less than 94 different RAF Squadrons had Blenheims on charge at some time or the other, more than any other type; or that they were used by over 210 other units, again more than any other type.

In common with most people, we thought Blenheims were used on operations just for the first few months of the war. We found that they were used operationally from the first sortie and the first bombing raid of the war in September 1939 right up to August 1943, and in non-operational units until after the end of the war. In fact the first squadron to be equipped with Blenheims — No 114 — was still soldiering on with them on operations over six years later! They were not alone for Nos 8, 34 and 139 Squadrons used them for over five years; whilst many other RAF Squadrons kept up operations on their Blenheims for over four years. This is a very long time indeed considering the wartime conditions of accelerated aircraft development and rapid deployment. So we discovered that Blenheims were employed far more extensively and for far, far longer than we had believed previously. Our eyes were being opened.

We learnt of the extreme bravery of the Blenheim crews. Of the three Victoria Crosses awarded to Blenheim pilots (compared with one for a Hurricane pilot and none for a Spitfire pilot) two were posthumous. Appropriately one VC went to a pilot of each of the three marks of Blenheim, and one was awarded in each Theatre of War: Wing Commander H.I. Edwards of 105 Squadron in a Mark IV in the European Theatre; Flight Lieutenant A.K.S. Scarf of 62 Squadron in a Mark I in the Far East; and Wing Commander H.G. Malcolm of 18 Squadron in a Mark V in the Middle East.

The courage of the 'Blenheim Boys' was legendary, the heavy losses appalling because they were inflicted, often quite needlessly, on the very cream of the RAF's small cadre of professional aircrew. The loss of so many experienced Section, Flight, Squadron and Base Commanders was particularly serious — indeed many of the relatively few Blenheim crews who survived the decimation of their Squadrons rose to the highest ranks of the Royal Air Force.

It has been my privilege to meet several of these gentlemen and persuade them to talk about their Blenheim days, an experience both humbling and enlightening. Most are still reluctant to 'shoot a line' and you almost have to drag from them tales of quite extraordinary courage. Some even feel guilty at having survived their Blenheim operations when so many of their friends and comrades, men that they considered finer and braver, did not. Many of these Blenheim survivors have been a source of inspiration to the team; their support and encouragement when the aircraft was destroyed so soon after the completion of the restoration was both immediate and invaluable.

Many have wondered just how the complete airworthy restoration of this long-neglected aircraft was undertaken and financed. Was it through one of the Services or national museums using public funds, as many felt it should have been? Was it restored at Filton by Bristol Aircraft Company, long absorbed into British Aerospace? Many, knowing that it was rebuilt at Duxford on the site of the Imperial War Museum, believed that the IWM were responsible for restoring the Blenheim. Or was it, like the private venture creation of the original prototype *Britain First* that lead to the whole Blenheim range, just left to private enterprise? In fact it was the latter in the shape of a small team of a dozen or so mainly volunteer enthusiasts who not only devoted so much of their time and effort to this unlikely-to-succeed project, but also maintained their great efforts throughout many years to a successful conclusion.

Many are curious as to what motivated them to overcome the immense difficulties involved. Some even asked, when the Blenheim finally flew again, 'Was it all worth it?' We think that it was. So much so that when the result of their endeavour was virtually destroyed within a month of its first flight, all of the team — without exception — volunteered immediately to do it all over again.

This was a quite extraordinary decision for them to make in the face of such a seemingly cruel blow from fate. For it was they who had given so much of their free time and hard work over the years in what can only be termed a labour of love. They had put so much of themselves into re-creating from an abandoned and decrepit shell of an airframe a beautiful, living, flying Blenheim, that their sense of deep personal loss at its sudden destruction can be well imagined. The whole team knew that there was nothing wrong with the aircraft; in fact it was better than new and performed perfectly. But it was completely and quite unnecessarily ruined in a few moments of recklessness by a pilot who really should have known better.

I will try and set before you just why they should react with such a positive determination to 'pick themselves up, dust themselves down, and start all over again' following the traumatic loss of their lovely, only recently completed Blenheim, for it was truly their pride and joy. But first I must provide an explanation as to just how I became so personally and heavily involved in what, but a few years ago, I would have regarded as the most unlikely sounding responsibility imaginable for me — that of restoring a completely dilapidated Blenheim hulk to perfect flying condition.

Like so many of the events in life that turn out later to be of great significance, indeed to change irrevocably the entire course of one's life, it all started quite by chance. Let me retrace how these chance meetings and the subsequent intertwining of seemingly quite unrelated developments led to a single Bristol Blenheim taking to the sky once more after over 40 years during which all the surviving examples had remained bound to terra firma. You will see how my heavy involvement in motor sport caused, most unexpectedly, aircraft to re-enter my life after a gap of over 20 years.

Aircraft, that is, in general, and the Blenheim in particular.

Chapter Two

The dream begins

For many years I had owned and run The Chequered Flag, a well-known garage in Chiswick, West London, that specialized in sports and Gran Turismo cars, and what are now termed classic cars although in those days they were just our normal stock in trade. The Flag had always supported motor racing or rallying, ostensibly for publicity purposes but really because I and those that worked there thoroughly enjoyed the involvement.

We ran racing teams for and with various manufacturers — F3 cars for Brabham and McLaren (in the days when they were run by Jack Brabham with Ron Taurenac, and Bruce McLaren with Teddy Mayer respectively) and GT cars for Lotus, the Elite-Climax and Elan-Cosworth; and two Shelby Cobras, a 289 (4.7 litre) and a 427 (7 litre). We also designed and built nearly 100 Gemini F3 racing cars. Jim Clark had his first ever single-seater race in a Chequered Flag Gemini, the first car ever to use a Ford-Cosworth engine. Jackie Stewart drove our racing Elans for a season, and Graham Hill drove our Lotus VII, XI and XV sports racing cars. These three future World Champions and many other famous drivers were helped on their way by driving for the Flag. We won the first 1,000 km race at Brands Hatch with a 7 litre Cobra — the only international race ever won by a Cobra — and numerous sports and GT races with various Lotus models.

I was lucky enough to win quite a few, mainly in Lotus GT cars, and to have driven at most of the Continental circuits as well as all those in the UK. I also enjoyed driving the works Aston-Martin Zagatos 1 VEV and 2 VEV, and was Jim Clark's team–mate on them in the Tourist Trophy at Goodwood. In the early 1960s, when I held the GT lap record at all the British circuits, racing was great fun and full of larger-than-life characters, and not as sophisticated and deadly serious as it has since become.

The Bristol Blenheim was then to me just the little-known name of an early

RAF bomber, forgotten by most people and of no particular interest to me. I had no idea that before very long it would come to dominate my life even more comprehensively than cars then did. For unknown to me, the links between me and the Blenheim were being forged in the mills of fate, if that's not too fanciful a phrase to describe the hidden process that rules our lives!

I had been interested in aircraft from an early age so I purchased a lovely little De Havilland Chipmunk from Mutt Summers, the Vickers Test Pilot. It was G-AKDN, the second prototype which he had entered in a couple of King's Cup air races, and I had it painted white with a black lower half to go with our racing cars. Someone once said 'The only difference between men and boys is the cost of their toys.' I got a private pilot's licence, which as an ex-RAF pilot was not too difficult, but I did not have time to enjoy it as much as I would have liked. Cars were central to my whole life, both work and play, at that time.

By the late 1960s I had 'hung up my helmet' as a driver so that I could concentrate on running the teams that we were so heavily involved with. The Flag progressed through teams of F3 and F2 McLarens, which were a complete disaster, and after far too many accidents one year we ended up building more McLarens than the factory itself!

Then we made an even bigger mistake and went into Formula 1, first to rescue the struggling Token Team and then with the ex-John Watson F1 Brabham, both with Ford Cosworth DFV engines. These were both driven by Ian Ashley who had shown great promise as a driver of Lola F5000 cars, winning the Gold Cup at Oulton Park in a car we had partly sponsored. But in the intense competition of Formula 1 he crashed more often than he qualified, and we just did not have the sponsorship and finance to compete with the big boys on anything like level terms.

That really was the end of the road as far as international motor racing and The Chequered Flag were concerned. I couldn't afford to let my heart rule my head any longer — indeed we had to work very hard for several years to make up the money we had lost through supporting motor racing. The Chipmunk was sold and I lost all interest in aviation.

But I missed motor sport. I missed the excitement, the noise and the spectacle; the mingling with the top teams and drivers, even the pressure of working to get the cars prepared by the deadline of the next event. I missed the travelling and the good food and wines on continental trips, and I missed the tremendous team spirit and close companionship that we had enjoyed.

Life was getting dull. It was insufficient just to run a business and make money; money is only a lubricant that makes life more comfortable. I feel that life needs to be lived to the full. So I was in a receptive frame of mind when Richard Banks, a public relations man with motor sport connections (and now a leading expert on restoring classic Alfa Romeos) came to see me in the mid 1970s and suggested that the Flag should re-enter motor sport via international rallies with the then sensational Italian supercar, the Lancia Stratos.

We put together a convincing prospectus and I went to Turin and managed to buy the only ex-factory Stratos to escape captivity, one of their Monte Carlo team cars. We engaged Per Inge Walfridsson, the leading available Swedish 'loose surface' driver, and Cahal Curley, the colourful Irish top 'tarmac' driver who had won the Circuit of Ireland, The Manx, etc, so things seemed most promising. The car blew an engine testing in Sweden, which we put down to oil surge, but when it went well it was quite fantastically fast. Life was looking interesting again.

Incidentally, my only experience of rallying had been 10 years earlier when I drove a works Reliant Sabre Six on the '64 Monte Carlo Rally. It had more power than the chassis could put down, we lost touch with our service crews, and it was bloody hard work. I drove the complete rally from the start at Glasgow to the finish at Monte Carlo, including all the special stages, entirely single-handed: my 'co-driver' would occasionally surface from his slumber and say 'Follow those cars' on the road sections and then at the start of the special stages fasten his harness a little tighter. He had filled me full of Benzedrine tablets and prohibited any liquid refreshment at all so I became very dehydrated. Meanwhile, our team-mate took his car the short way down a steep mountainside by overturning across several lacets that linked a series of hairpins and reducing his car to shredded wheat.

It was not my idea of fun trying to drive fast when extremely fatigued over often icy mountain passes and little unmade tracks in the middle of nowhere, frequently with just the odd white-painted stone to mark the edge of a very long drop into the valleys below. However, I digress.

Richard was right. The Flag obtained widespread publicity through campaigning the exciting Stratos, and in fact became the leading Lancia agent in the UK largely as a result. As a small private team we took on the might of the works teams and their top drivers from all the major motor manufacturers, and had the support of thousands of spectators who always seem to like the underdogs. Literally millions of people see an event like the RAC Rally and rallying received quite good television coverage. Our hard work seemed justified.

The car looked and sounded absolutely magnificent while it was still going. We led many international rallies but lasted to win just a few — Mintex, Donegal, Ulster. Tony Pond wrapped it round a tree 18 ft from the ground, Cahal rolled it to a ball in Donegal, Per crashed badly when leading the 1975 Welsh and the car was burnt out. We brought back from Kenya a Stratos driven into the ground by the factory team while recce-ing the African Safari Rally, and tried again, but the car always flattered only to deceive. *Autosport* headed a feature on the Flag Stratos 'The dream that became a nightmare'.

We tried with an ex-Works Porsche 3 litre RS and a Leyland factory-backed Triumph TR8, but they were always just off the pace, and several serious and expensive accidents later with no hope of winning anything important, we realized that we just could not continue. It seemed then, by the late 1970s, that the long involvement of The Chequered Flag with motor sport had finally come to an end.

Just then Robs Lamplough reappeared on the scene. I had known him slightly back in his Formula 3 days, when Frank Williams led a band of racing reprobates that included Piers Courage, Chris Irwin, Charlie Creighton-

Above *Robs Lamplough in action at Brands Hatch in the BRM that formed the first link between Graham Warner and the Blenheim.*

Above right *The Blenheim components as I first saw them, laying in a hangar at Duxford; a derelict nose, the rear fuselage of 9893, and the centre-sections. Part-restored B17 and B25 are visible in the other half of the hangar.*

Stewart, Charles Lucas and Co from a notorious North London flat. They didn't win much, but always enjoyed their racing to the full. Robs said he was racing a front-engined P25 BRM in historic races and persuaded me to sponsor him for a couple of seasons, for a modest sum, which I agreed to. I will admit that I was influenced by the fact that he was building up another P25 BRM, owned several other fascinating cars including a front–engined Ferrari Testa Rossa, and had dangled the prospect of some very tempting drives in vintage or historic races before me. I heard him muttering that he had some 'pretty interesting' aircraft too, but I didn't pay very much attention to this. Perhaps I should have done!

We tested the BRM a couple of times and he drove it very well in several races for historic cars. It couldn't be finished in our traditional black-and-white colour scheme as it had to race in the correct original silvery shade of British Racing Green, so it carried the Flag logo on the scuttle.

It was entered in the historic car race which supported the British Grand Prix at Silverstone. As there is usually a traffic problem at Silverstone during the Grand Prix weekend I was delighted when Robs offered to take me there in his Harvard. He collected me at Booker (Wycombe Air Park) and we had to jump the queue a bit to land on the runway in the centre of Silverstone 'spot on'

our allocated time slot — people were calling 'finals' just before their time slot irrespective of whether they even had Silverstone in sight!

We had a good day's racing and I met quite a few old friends so didn't feel completely cut-off from motor sport. As we left, Robs did the odd roll for the amusement of the queues of traffic. When he dropped me back at Booker he said, 'You must come up to Duxford some time and see my Spitfires and Mustangs.' I agreed, and noted the plurals. To be frank I took this with a pinch of salt as not many people actually do own Spitfires and Mustangs!

I rang Duxford Airfield, which was an outstation of the Imperial War Museum at Lambeth, and at that time used mainly for storage, and asked if they knew a Mr Lamplough. 'Oh yes,' they said. 'He is restoring several aircraft here, including a few Spitfires and two ex-Israeli Mustangs.'

So early in 1979 I went with Robs to Duxford. We climbed over a pile of aluminium scrap in a old hut, amongst which I could just about recognize bits of Spitfire — he assured me they were the components of three complete airframes recovered from the Golan Heights, and were awaiting restoration. This seemed an almost impossible task to me. Similarly, in another hut, were two very sorry-looking P51D Mustang fuselages and another huge pile of bits and pieces. Amazingly enough, 10 years later, he now flies one of the Mustangs, and at least two of the Spitfires were restored and are now airworthy!

In a hangar he had a Russian Yak 11 advanced trainer, which had force-landed in Cyprus on its way to Egypt, which was at least a more or less complete aircraft. In the back corner of this hangar was the derelict and very battered remains of what I recognized as the front and rear fuselage sections of an old

Early stages. A wing (inverted) in the 'shop; the aileron, tank-bay cover, outer flap and wing-tip are missing. The partly paint-stripped fuselage of 10038 is on trestles to the right.

Bristol Blenheim. I only knew that because it had the characteristic and oddly scalloped asymmetric Blenheim long nose which I remembered from old photographs last seen very many years before in my Air Scout and Air Training Corps days. Aircraft recognition had been one of the few subjects that I was any good at as a lad!

The dusty and vandalized wreck, a mixture of battered, bare, dulled alloy and very faded yellow paint, lay on some old tyres, together with two centre sections, with the undercarriage and rusty engine-mounts, stacked against the wall in a corner. I thought that the remains belonged to the IWM and were destined for eventual rebuild as a static exhibit for the main Lambeth Museum, though even that looked a difficult and daunting undertaking.

These Blenheim components meant nothing much to me in the context of the many aircraft and parts of aircraft in different stages of dereliction and restoration, scattered throughout Duxford. I had no affinity with, or particular interest in Blenheims at all. However, unbeknown to me, a Blenheim had entered my life although I did not, and could not, at that stage realize just how inextricably our futures were to be entwined.

On that fateful day at Duxford, Robs and I wandered past another workshop, locked and forlorn with several broken windows and a little notice saying 'Blenheim Palace' on the door. It was Building 66, and through the windows we could see the second example of what was clearly a pair with the Blenheim in the hangar, similarly derelict front and rear fuselage sections.

However, this one was mounted on trestles and had been partly paint-stripped, and the interior was virtually gutted. The shop was full of piles of scrappy looking bits and pieces, mainly dented and damaged alloy but some rusty steel engine frames too, and coils of dirty cables and broken wiring. Visible through the windows of the next hut was a heap of about 20 very rusty and badly corroded radial engines, and mounds of battered and corroded alloy panels, and various other bits and pieces that looked as if they had come from a scrapyard.

I asked Robs what was happening with it all for it appeared to have been abandoned. He said that nothing was happening to it as it was a project that had ground to a complete stop as the previous owner had been killed in an aircraft accident. This was a purely casual enquiry, although Robs knew I was an ex-RAF pilot and still had a vestigal interest in aeroplanes, and I may have told him my eldest brother had been in the RAF during the war.

We repaired to 'The Chequers', an appositely named inn in nearby Fowlmere, where I admired the photos of Thunderbolts and Mustangs from

'Blenheim Palace' laid out for Duxford's first open day in 1978. From the left: port wing and fuselage stern section (both inverted), fin (seen end-on), pair of undercarriage legs, and pilot's seat. Rear fuselage of 10038 to the right.

Americans who had been based with the 78th Fighter Group at Duxford and its satellite airfield at Fowlmere during the war. Robs was full of enthusiasm about restoring and flying his old aircraft and tried to convince me that it was a 'scene' that I would not only enjoy but would also be very good at. He said it had added a new dimension to his life and thought it would do the same for me. Prophetic words! The food and wine were certainly good, and the lunch most interesting as I asked Robs to tell me all that he knew about the battered bits of the two Blenheims that we had seen at Duxford that morning.

In the back of my mind the intriguing idea was forming that I might get involved in some sort of rescue attempt. It seemed to me a great shame that the Blenheim restoration project had been abandoned, and was most unlikely to be resurrected. Even at that very early stage I felt that it was far too important an aircraft, and of too much historic significance to the RAF, to allow it thus to fade almost entirely from the public memory. From being a virtually forgotten bomber it appeared likely to become a completely forgotten bomber.

I believed that the Blenheim deserved to be preserved and remembered. But was it important enough really to be worth rescuing and restoring? If no-one else was going to do it — and it appeared that they were not — should I? Could I? Was it even possible?

Chapter Three

The Blenheim team

Having explained how my long involvement in motor racing had the most unlikely result of leading me back to my earlier but long-lost interest in aviation matters and the Blenheim, I must now explain how during my formative years my keen interest in aircraft in general, and the wartime RAF in particular, had been aroused in the first place.

The youngest of three boys in a family that had no aviation connections at all, I followed my elder brothers into the Scouts. My eldest brother was Troop Leader then Assistant Scout Master, so I had always looked up to him. In 1941, as soon as he was old enough, he volunteered for pilot training with the RAF. We were all very proud of him. He grew quieter after his training was completed and once explained to me that he might go back to his unit from leave one day and not be able to return home again, either for a very long time, or possibly ever. I was far too young to understand what he was trying to prepare me for.

He either had a premonition or was just facing up to an inescapable truth for those in Bomber Command at that time, for he did not come back. His life was lost returning from a raid on Stettin in April 1943, shot down in a 102 Squadron Halifax MkII near the Danish coast. He was barely 20 years old, his name was Alex, but his RAF nickname was 'Plum', after Sir Pelham Warner the pre-war cricketer. I was a small boy, and thought the world of him, so his loss upset me greatly. I found it hard to accept that I would never actually see, hear or touch him again; that his gentle smile, now frozen photographically in perpetuity, would never soften his living face again. I did not then realize that with the passing of the years even he would become just a distant memory.

That is how at a very impressionable age I came to read all I could about the RAF in general and Bomber Command in particular, mainly from the collection of aviation books that Alex left to me. This gave me a good background knowledge of the aircraft they flew and just an inkling of what the crews had to endure in the course of their operations.

I formed an Air Scout Patrol in our troop, became troop leader myself, joined the Air Training Corps too and rose to Flight Sergeant by the time I was 16. I gained 'air experience', as they called the flights we cadged at ATC camps on RAF airfields. Although the war had been over some years by then, I was determined to follow in my brother's footsteps and joined the Air Force when I was old enough. I was awarded my 'wings' when just 19, after completing my flying training at 4 FTS in Rhodesia (as it was then) on Harvards, and then flew Meteors and Vampires back in the UK.

But when I visited Duxford all those years later, all this aviation knowledge and interest, even Alex's very memory, had faded almost completely away like the foreign languages learnt at school. I knew that he had flown Tiger Moths initially, Ansons and Whitleys at OTU, and then Halifaxes at the 4 Group Heavy Conversion Unit and on the operational Squadron at Driffield and Pocklington. As far as I know he had no connections with Blenheims at all.

Had the sad remains in the back of the hangar been those of a Whitley or Halifax my interest in a possible restoration as a static exhibit of either would have been aroused, especially as I knew that there were no complete surviving examples of either aircraft anywhere in the world, and I felt strongly that there should be. I was conscious that post-war generations did not understand or appreciate the sheer size and the great cost, both in industrial and in human terms, of the Bomber Command offensive.

At that stage — even with my personal and special interest in Bomber Command — I certainly failed to appreciate either the scale or the proportionally far greater cost of the almost sacrificial Blenheim operations throughout the first three years of the war. My eyes were to be opened to the extreme extent of both, and as my own understanding of the Blenheim's true role grew I became more determined to try and open the eyes of others too.

But I'm getting ahead of the story of this particular Blenheim; for it was only later, as the research undertaken to ensure a completely authentic Blenheim restoration proceeded, that this determination became for me almost a crusade. As the physical restoration of our Blenheim progressed and grew, so did my personal aim to ensure that the true historical importance of the Bristol Blenheim, long belittled or almost ignored by historians, should become properly recognized.

Robs knew the owner of the Blenheim components at Duxford and gave me the telephone number of Wensley Haydon-Baillie, a highly successful businessman who was acting for the estate of his late brother, Ormond Haydon-Baillie. Wensley, whose extra business interests were with Naval not Aviation affairs, was even then in the process of disposing of his late brother's aircraft collection, so the timing was most fortuitous. I arranged to go and see him to discuss the possible acquisition of the abandoned Blenheim project.

Ormond apparently had been a very charismatic and enterprising man, and was also a dashing and very good pilot, very popular at air displays. He had purchased the Blenheim remains for a fairly nominal sum from Wes Agnew in

Three of the youngsters in front of Haydon-Baillie's T33 at Duxford. Two of course are still there — 'Beans' works with Marshalls at Cambridge airport.

Manitoba whilst he had been an RAF Flight Lieutenant seconded to the RCAF a few years earlier.

He had initially purchased á Hawker Sea Fury and entered it in the Reno Air Races, then ferrying it back to England. Later he purchased two Lockheed T33s, advanced Jet Trainers, and added an Avro-Canada CF100, a Gloster Meteor Mk 8, a de Havilland Chipmunk and some North American F86 Sabres. Clearly the collecting bug had bitten him deeply!

Ormond formed the 'Black Knight' Air Display Team and based his aircraft at Duxford, which was a famous but then deserted ex-RAF airfield near Cambridge, which had lain unused and going to rack and ruin whilst the various authorities decided what to do with it. The Imperial War Museum arranged with the MOD to store some of their overflow collection from Lambeth there as an outstation, but the site was not open to the public.

Ormond just commandeered empty buildings to house his growing collection.

He gathered a team of young aircraft enthusiasts about him who were willing in their spare time to assist him clean, maintain and operate these exciting aircraft. They formed the nucleus of the later Blenheim team. He organized a trip to India and brought back several very dilapidated Spitfire airframes which had been, quite literally, put out to grass on Indian airfields as decoy aircraft during the India/Pakistan War, and just left there. He intended to restore one or more to flying condition.

Ormond wished to restore one of the Blenheims as well, and the least damaged fuselage sections of one were put in an empty hut, and the volunteers started gutting the interior and stripping the external paint from it. That was as far as the restoration had proceeded when I took it over. The team also replaced most of the broken windows in the hut and rigged up some shelves and benches. The hut was christened 'Blenheim Palace', but officially is called Building 66, and is still used by the team to this day.

There were always plenty of jobs to do on the other aircraft so the work on the Blenheim project had a low priority and little was actually done. It seems unlikely that the Blenheim restoration would have seen through to the end, and even more unlikely that it would be completed to airworthy standards. We will never know for, full of enthusiasm for his latest acquisition from an Italian of a superbly restored P51D 'Mustang', Ormond made that one fatal error during an air display in Germany, crashed and was killed. Tragically a hero-worshipping German teenager who 'went for the ride' was killed with him.

As one of the team said, 'It was just as if the light went out.' All Ormond's inspired leadership, all his collector's drive, all his direction and guidance of the team was gone. The team drifted away, his various aircraft sat forlornly at Duxford awaiting their fate, the Blenheim components gathered more dust. It seemed that the planned restoration could not now go ahead.

The IWM needed the space as the Duxford site was by then open to the public and the exhibits were expanding rapidly. They had numerous other items they wished to put on show, many months had gone by since Ormond's death, and Wensley was asked ever more forcefully to remove the aircraft, including the Blenheims. But there had never been a formal tenancy or loan agreement with the IWM that could be enforced or terminated, so an unsatisfactory stalemate ensued.

This was the situation I had to resolve. I had obtained from Wensley a list of the Black Knight team members and arranged to meet them all in The Chequers one evening. They were a great bunch, cheerful and enthusiastic, and readily agreed that they would continue to work on the Blenheim if the project would be seen right through to completion. Perhaps I appeared to them like the proverbial White Knight coming to the rescue!

I got a key to Blenheim Palace and inspected what I could — what a monumental task it would be! I went round it all again with Fred Hanson, the most experienced, almost revered, fully licenced aircraft engineer who had been keeping an official eye on the project. I needed his agreement that it *was* possible to restore the remains to airworthy condition (for I decided that I was

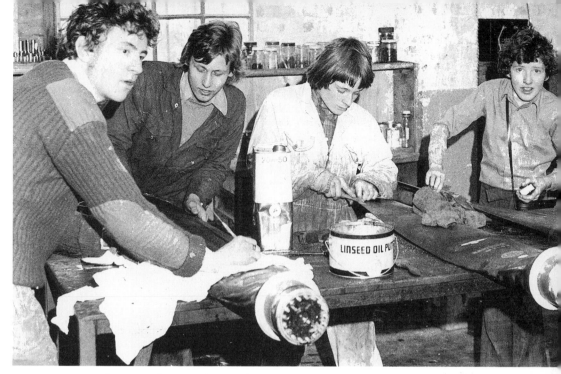

Some of Haydon-Baillie's team of young enthusiasts cleaning Blenheim prop blades: 'Beans' Smith, Robert Jackson, John Romain and Billy Kelly.

The pile of unrestored parts at Duxford. A pair of tailplanes and elevators at the rear, turrets to the right, two rudders in the centre, and axle and brake shoes left front at the base of the pile. Note the inscription on the turret dated 23/4/1943.

not interested in a mere static restoration), but he was reluctant to give it. Gradually I overcame his long list of objections and (ever the optimist) said 'If man made it once, man can make it again' and 'Where there's a will there's a way' and similar fatuous remarks.

He was not impressed, and felt I had no idea just what a monumental task I was taking on, but finally agreed that 'as long as I had a bottomless pocket' it could be done. I could justify putting the whole restoration project through the garage company so did not anticipate that the funding would prove too difficult, for we could control the rate of work and the purchase of materials, therefore regulating the level of expenditure.

I had been told that the two derelict airframes at Duxford were in fact Bolingbrokes, the name the Canadians gave to the Bristol Type 149 Mk IV 'Long Nose' Blenheim built under licence from Bristol Aircraft Co by Fairchild Aircraft Co in Canada during the war. This back-up production was arranged in case the parent Bristol factory at Filton or the Rootes 'shadow' factory were put out of action by German bombing. Similar arrangements were made at that time for the licensed production in Canada of Hawker Hurricanes and Westland Lysanders, with Avro Lancasters and de Havilland Mosquitos following later in the war. Both British factories had the Type 149 Mk IV 'long nose' Blenheim in full series production, as this model had followed the Type 142 Mk I 'short nose' Blenheim on the production lines before the war. The Rootes factory later built some 1,000 of the Type 160 Blenheim Mk V, known initially as the Bisley.

Incidentally, as Bristol Type 149s were identical whether built in England or Canada, apart from minor differences in instrumentation, I always have and always will refer to the Duxford examples as Blenheims — the lay public are already sufficiently confused about the Blenheim/Bolingbroke/Bisley naming complexities that I like to concentrate their attention solely on Blenheims. The static Blenheim on display in the RAF museum at Hendon is also technically a Bolingbroke, but only the pedantic still use that name.

Altogether well over 6,000 Blenheims of the three types were built, of all these only a handful — all licence-built Mk IV examples — had survived as static exhibits in a few museums, but not a single example anywhere in the world was airworthy or ever likely to become so.

Just like the Halifax, Stirling, Hampden, Manchester and Whitley, of which not a single complete example of any existed anywhere, and the Wellington of which there was only one in the RAF museum (before the remains of another — now in the Brooklands Museum — was dredged up from the depths of Loch Ness), the Blenheim had been ill-served by those who should have been responsible for preserving examples of these significant wartime RAF bombers.

I felt that our national aviation heritage had been sadly neglected when examples of such important aircraft were not preserved but simply allowed to fade into obscurity, and this feeling undoubtedly influenced me in deciding to rescue the Blenheim restoration project.

At that time there was only one airworthy example extant of the famous Lancaster, that operated by the RAF's Memorial Flight, until the Canadian

Warplane Heritage more recently completed the restoration of their example. The fact that there are now two airworthy Lancasters, both displayed at air shows, helps to perpetuate their fame to the extent that the average man in the street seems to remember only the Lancaster when asked about Bomber Command wartime aircraft. Clearly displaying a restored Bristol Blenheim at air shows would help put the Blenheim back on the map and redress the balance.

Several meetings with Wensley and his factotum Roger Sweet followed to establish just what was at Duxford, for no inventory existed, and to agree a price fair to both parties. An exchange of drafts with the IWM to formalize the working arrangement and the terms of the long-term loan agreement was put in hand. After lengthy negotiations with both Ted Inman, The Keeper at Duxford, who was most helpful, and Dr Noble Frankland, the IWM Director General at Lambeth, agreement was reached. A sales contract with the Haydon-Baillie Estate soon followed.

The Blenheim restoration project had been rescued; the Blenheim team re-formed, and remotivated. A Blenheim *would* fly again!

Chapter Four

British Aerial Museum

Now work on making a Blenheim fit to fly again could commence in earnest. Many aviation experts shook their heads and said that it just couldn't be done. We were determined that it would be, so we started organizing things with that one end in view. The airframe and available components were thoroughly surveyed and a rebuilding programme initiated.

To give the ex-Black Knight team a fresh identity (and to have a name designed to look better to the aviation industry, various authorities, and some of the overseas museums we would have to deal with) we called ourselves The British Aerial Museum, with the sub-title 'of Flying Military Aircraft' to show that we conserved and operated airworthy as opposed to merely static aircraft. A new BAM logo of a three-bladed propeller enhanced our blue letterhead, and the team wore it on their new overalls too. The revitalized team was off to a good start.

The workshops at 'Blenheim Palace' were equipped with a range of workshop equipment and tools, decent lighting, a compressed-air system, benches, shelves, etc, and the stores, office and crew-room were fitted out. However, there was no heating in the workshops until several years later so the fact that the team left the warmth of their homes to continue working throughout the winter months gives an idea of their dedication to the restoration. An enjoyable Christmas dinner (enlivened considerably by items from the joke shop) for the whole team, and their wives and girlfriends held that first winter started a happy tradition that we have been glad to maintain since.

As you have seen, the circumstances that led to the restoration of a flying Blenheim were complex and unusual. It was necessary to give some detail as to how I became involved in the first place, what originally aroused my interest in aircraft, what motivated me to undertake the restoration and how I remotivated the rest of the Blenheim team. It is now necessary to give some background to the relationship, also complex and unusual, between our team and the Imperial War Museum.

Some people think that, because our operation is based at Duxford with the Imperial War Museum, we are an offshoot of the IWM itself; at one Duxford Air Display I was even told that BAM was funded by the Government! I must make it clear that we are a small private organization, utilizing facilities provided by the IWM on a strictly commercial basis, but unfortunately we are not the recipients of *any* financial support from the IWM or any other Government institution, department or branch of the Armed Forces.

The IWM's brief is to 'tell the story of warfare in the twentieth century where it involved the United Kingdom and her Empire, Commonwealth or Allies'. Thus both Lambeth and Duxford contain many items, large and small, of military and naval equipment, weapons, uniforms, etc, as well as documents, films, photographs and paintings, so the aircraft and aviation exhibits represent but one aspect of this. The IWM is also responsible for HMS *Belfast*, a cruiser moored in the Thames, and the Cabinet War Rooms beneath Whitehall, both of which are open to the public.

The actual arrangement at Duxford is very sensible: the IWM provides workshops and hangar space for the restoration and operation of suitable ex-military aircraft owned by private owners or organizations such as ours, in return for long-term loan agreements to put the aircraft on show to the public as exhibits. Additionally all the privately owned aircraft based at Duxford are required to contribute a series of air displays there free of charge, to earn their keep, as it were.

This unusual co-operation between private enterprise and a national museum works very well in practice and has undoubtedly helped Duxford to become not only the major aircraft collection in Europe but also unique as a museum in offering visitors the rare opportunity to see at such close quarters old military aircraft in their true element — actually taking to the air.

The privately owned aircraft have to be relevant to the IWM's theme and finished in authentic military colours and markings, and are selected carefully as with the growing success of the arrangement pressure on space at Duxford has grown too. They also participate in air displays at other venues, and do film and photographic work, plus air-tests, pilot conversions, continuation training, etc, so there is nearly always some flying or engine running going on at Duxford to add to the interest and enjoyment of visitors.

This constant flying activity by the private owners is crucial to the undoubted attraction of Duxford as an entertaining and informative venue for a family day out, for it keeps the airfield alive and thus sets Duxford apart from the usual static museums that appeal only to dedicated enthusiasts. That this uncommon blend of active and static exhibits — for as well as aircraft some of the tanks and military vehicles on show also burst into life at intervals — is highly successful in attracting visitors to Duxford is shown by the increasing numbers of public attendances. These now number well over 400,000 per year — many of whom find the site so fascinating that they return time and time again.

When the British Aerial Museum was formed originally at Duxford the privately owned aircraft there were only the Boeing B17 Fortress 'Sally B'; Robs's Harvard, Yak 11, Staggerwing, Pilatus P2 and his various aircraft under restoration; an early Auster; Mike Russell's aircraft including a Rapide and Tiger Moth being rebuilt; plus another Rapide and a Proctor under restoration.

Now there is The Old Flying Machine Co of Ray Hanna and his son Mark, with Spitfire, Mustang, Corsair, P40, Avenger, Buchon (a Spanish licence-built Messerschmitt Bf 109), Harvard, etc; The Fighter Collection of Stephen Grey, a magnificent collection of a dozen rare fighter aircraft and a B25 Mitchell; Plain Sailing with their Catalina, Tigercat and Pilatus P2; and Lindsay Walton with his Corsair, Stearman and Me 108. So with BAM's six airworthy aircraft there are currently over 30 flying aircraft, plus another eight or nine under restoration to fly, based at Duxford.

Unfortunately some of the earlier private-owner residents have had to be weeded out, including Robs Lamplough's collection which is now at North Weald, but Duxford still has an unrivalled collection of rare airworthy ex-military aircraft. When these and the civil airliners of the Duxford Aviation Society are added to the IWM's own impressive collection the result is well over 100 interesting aircraft on show.

It must be explained that up to now aircraft of the IWM's own collection are not allowed to fly in case they should be destroyed as a result of a flying

Below   *The derelict airframe of RCAF 10038 standing in the field at Manitoba where it had lain out in all weathers for 40 years. Note the faded red, white and blue markings on the fin, and the vestigal remains of the rudder and elevators.*

Below right   *Laying out the battered components, partially dismantled during the recovery operation, ready for shipment to the UK.*

accident. The exception is a Hawker Sea Hurricane, which was left to the Shuttleworth Collection and which they and the IWM are restoring jointly to airworthy condition at Duxford to be operated from there when completed. Incidentally, the building next to 'Blenheim Palace' where the Sea Hurricane is being rebuilt was the engine and prop shop for the first Blenheim restoration, and we gave it up on completion but now wish we still had the use of it!

I hope that this has put the Blenheim restoration into the proper context *vis-à-vis* the set-up at Duxford, and explained the relationship between our British Aerial Museum team and the Imperial War Museum. All our team are members of the Duxford Aviation Society who supply the volunteers to the various conservation and restoration tasks at Duxford, and even when we recruit additional members direct they still have to join the DAS. We are happy to co-operate with this arrangement, and indeed BAM has a group membership of DAS to facilitate this co-operation.

Incidentally, the Duxford Aviation Society both owns and preserves the range of civil airliners, including the Concorde, that are exhibited statically at Duxford. Although these are beyond the remit of the War Museum they certainly deserve to be preserved and provide a further area of great interest to aviation minded visitors.

Even given the enthusiasm of the BAM team, the workshops and other facilities made available by the IWM, and the equipment and finance provided by my garage company, how realistic were the chances of actually completing the restoration? What were the problems that faced the team at the start of a total rebuild of the sad remains of a wartime aircraft back to 'as new' flying condition once more? Was it all just a pipe-dream? Many thought so.

We had only the damaged, derelict and dilapidated hulk of an airframe that had stood outside through nearly 40 severe Canadian winters, had been

stripped of many parts, and had lost most of its complex systems, the cockpit in particular being completely demolished. Children had used it as a plaything, and for target practice; farmers had removed anything useful. The pile of engines were virtual scrap, being seized solid, often damaged and all very badly corroded. The whole airframe had suffered vandalism and severe general deterioration over this long period, and had been home to various birds, plants and rodents. Not a promising start for a rebuild to airworthy status!

The aircraft had originally been designed in the early 1930s, and the supercharged Mercury engines were a development of the unsupercharged Jupiter range which had its origins in the First World War. All the technology employed was completely out of date, very labour-intensive, and far removed from current aviation engineering practice. Some of the materials used in the original construction were no longer obtainable. Blenheims were mass-produced quickly in wartime with a very short life expectancy and were certainly not built, or even intended, to last for anything like 40 or 50 years.

Many essential items and components were either missing completely or far too damaged to be salvageable. We had no drawings or plans, no spare parts were available. The Bristol Aircraft Company at Filton had been swallowed by British Aerospace, and Bristol Engines Division had disappeared too, into Rolls-Royce Aircraft Engines Ltd. We as a team had no previous experience of such a mammoth undertaking. No wonder most people said it just couldn't be done.

But it *was* done. Each difficulty and obstacle, however apparently insurmountable or even apparently terminal, was overcome or circumvented successfully, and I will try to describe and illustrate exactly how in the next few chapters.

The brunt of the sustained hard work and the ingenious solving of each difficulty as it arose, was borne entirely by the team themselves — no praise is too high for their constant endeavour and enterprise. Without their unstinting efforts and dedication it is certain that this Blenheim would not have flown again. I am proud to know them, I am glad to lead them, I count them all as friends — I hope I am worthy of them.

What makes ordinary people accept such a daunting challenge and be so willing to tackle such a seemingly impossible task? What sort of person actually volunteers for this most demanding undertaking? Why do they then devote so much of their spare time over so many years — for they all have to cope with ordinary jobs as well — to such an unlikely objective as making a Blenheim fit to fly once more? I will try to answer these questions too, though I am still often surprised at and humbled by the depth of their devotion and dedication to the Blenheim.

Chapter Five

Meet the team

The original crew chief of the volunteers in Ormond Haydon-Baillie's day was John Gullick, a great aviation enthusiast who was a skilled printer by trade, later moving on to Marconi on the missile side. He had been a Flight Observer in the Army Air Corps, serving in Cyprus during the emergency. Slightly older than the rest of the team, he led the expedition to India to rescue the derelict Spitfires for Ormond. He was a solid and conscientous team leader, well respected and liked by the team, who could turn his hand most ably to virtually any job on the restoration, apart from electrics which were as much a mystery to him as they are to most people!

Gullick made an enormous contribution to the first restoration and was a steadying influence on the team, even though he would often get that 'far away' look in his eyes when an attractive girl passed the workshops, much to the team's amusement. So it was a serious loss when his new job took him down to the south coast.

It says much for his strength of character that when John Romain, a much younger volunteer member of the team, came to work full-time on the project on the completion of his aeronautical engineering apprenticeship with British Aerospace at Hatfield, and was later appointed Chief Engineer, that John Gullick accepted the reversal of roles and continued to work on the restoration just as hard and diligently.

After several years as a part-time volunteer, John Romain joined the Blenheim team full-time as a fully trained and skilled aircraft engineer in July 1980. He not only studied for and gained his CAA engineering licences, but also his private pilot's licence, and he has become a very competent pilot indeed, displaying most of our collection of ex-Military aircraft with distinction at various airshows. He has now taken his Commercial Pilot's Licence, and is a director of Aircraft Restorations Ltd, trading under our new title of The

Aircraft Restoration Company — a name which better describes our activities.

Possessed of a keen and lively intelligence as well as a cheerful, ingenuous and outgoing personality, he soon became the cornerstone of the whole Blenheim restoration programme and chief engineer on the project. No one worked harder or longer, and certainly no one understood the practical difficulties involved in the restoration better, or devised more ingenious ways of overcoming them.

He has been heavily involved in rebuilding the Blenheim from the beginning to the end, indeed almost half his entire life has been spent on it, and now he is doing it all over again!

Previously known as 'Little John' for he's not very tall (and to help differentiate between the four Johns on the team), he has a pleasant, open manner and easy grin, plus the good fortune of looking far younger than he is. No one at Duxford is more universally popular than John Romain. The first restoration could not have been completed without his selfless dedication, the constant application of his many skills and the vast amount of sheer hard work he put in over such a long period. If a Distinguished Service Order could be awarded in the aircraft restoration movement, he certainly deserves one!

For him to have to sit there alongside the pilot who destroyed this priceless aircraft at Denham — to see the accident coming and be unable to prevent it — must have been truly terrible. Priceless not in monetary terms but in terms of the immense human effort that had gone into the Blenheim over so many years. Terrible in the sense that it was an awful, dreadful, traumatic experience that John of all people should not have had to undergo.

John is married to Amanda, the attractive younger sister of Robert Jackson, one of Ormond's original team. Robert, now married too, had to take over his father's building business on the latter's retirement and unfortunately can no longer spare the time to work on the Blenheim, but we still see him from time to time.

When John and Amanda were married at the beautiful village church in Whittlesford, the vicar in his address reminded the congregation that John was already married to a Bristol Blenheim and that a lot of tolerance and understanding would be needed. It certainly was for as the Blenheim was approaching the first flight John worked for an incredible number of hours, often very late into the night. As the bridal couple left the church 'Hoof' Proudfoot performed a slow roll overhead in a Spitfire, which was a nice touch.

Amanda is now an air hostess with Air UK, so flying is in her blood too. They live at Linton, near team-member John Larcombe, in a delightful old thatched cottage where anyone over 5ft 6in has to duck to avoid the beams!

Absolute stalwarts of the volunteer team are the Swann brothers, Colin and David, originally from Fowlmere. Both are highly skilled and very versatile aircraft engineers who do shift work — Colin works for British Aerospace at Hatfield and David has been with Monarch Airlines at Luton for 12 years — so they can put in several days a week on the Blenheim at Duxford, plus every Sunday along with the rest of the team. Their wives are even longer-suffering than so-called golf widows.

John and Colin replacing the repaired tank-bay panel which fits between the spars on the under surface of the wing.

Colin is an ex–RAF Halton apprentice, and although these trainees are known colloquially as 'brats', they undergo the very best general aviation engineering training. He is very good on electrical systems and in fact designed the special electrical layout on the Blenheim which was a cunning blend of the old original 12 volt system and more modern avionics. David too is an ex-aircraft engineering apprentice with Marshalls of Cambridge, and is now fully licensed.

Both Colin and David can turn their hands to anything from paint-stripping, metalwork and alloy repairs to making and riveting new skins, but their speciality is the systems installations — hydraulic, pneumatic, flying and engine controls, electrics and instruments — and 'plumbing' the engines with fuel and oil circuits. These systems are the very heart of an aircraft and take a lot of time and application to get right, because they have to be made perfectly, rigorously tested, and carefully adjusted if they all are to function correctly. It says a lot for the very high standard of the work of the team as a whole, but of Colin and David in particular, that all the systems did function perfectly when the time came and the Blenheim was airborne!

David is also very adept at applying aircraft markings and is an able signwriter, as is Hugh Smith, an aircraft electrical engineer with Qualitair at Stansted, whose main speciality is wiring and aircraft electrical systems, and who did a lot of very good work on these systems on the Blenheim with Colin. Hugh had been an aircraft engineer but had to leave the industry during a recession and became a telephone engineer, keeping in touch with aircraft by his work on the Blenheim. He is now back in the aviation industry full time and much happier for it!

Hugh and David, with their careful research and meticulous attention to detail, ensure that the national and squadron markings, plus the individual aircraft lettering, serial number, stencils, etc, on our collection of ex-military aircraft are all correctly placed, styled and coloured. Hugh is a very good maker of scale model aircraft and said that applying the markings to our aircraft is just like working on full-size models!

Flypast picture of David Swann, John Romain in the cockpit, and John 'Smudge' Smith, taken in 'Blenheim Palace' in 1981. Smudge is justifiably proud of his newly fabricated firewall.

All who have visited 'Blenheim Palace' at Duxford cannot fail to have noticed the ever-cheerful countenance and friendly manner of John Smith, universally known as 'Smudger', a nickname from his RAF days when he was a skilled metal worker, serving mainly in Germany. He went on to research work with the Ministry of Aviation, and his present job with the Hertfordshire Police Force is very demanding. Behind his jovial personality and fund of jokes lies a serious and very hard-working man who is absolutely dedicated to the Blenheim restoration.

Good 'metal-bashers', especially those able to work well with old alloy, are few and far between and the team is most fortunate that 'Smudger' spends so much time at Duxford, for he not only keeps us all amused but his input into the myriad metal-working jobs on the Blenheim airframe restoration is also of immense importance.

'Smudger' has straightened and repaired innumerable bent bits of the aircraft structure, fabricating replacements if they were beyond repair; he has welded, panel-beaten and planished alloy panels, as well as making many new panels and fairings; but above all he had drilled out tens of thousands of rivets, re-drilled each hole and re-riveted each one with a new rivet. Without his crucial contribution the Blenheim rebuild would have taken far, far longer to complete.

He was the third crew member when the aircraft crashed at Denham, not as some reports have stated a passenger 'just along for the ride'. As a relic of its wartime service the Blenheim had all its electrical controls such as master-switch, ameters, charging-rate controls, battery-isolating switches, etc, placed alongside the dorsal turret where they were originally operated by the WOP/AG (Wireless Operator/Air Gunner) and we had reinstated them in the correct position.

Another long-serving and key member of the team is William Kelly, known as Billy, who started working as a volunteer at Duxford when still in his very early teens, when he was a bit of a tearaway, and he has been working there ever since. Since 1988 this has become a full-time rather than a part-time job, after several years as a mobile refrigeration and air-conditioning engineer, and he is now very knowledgeable on aircraft and a first-class restorer.

He completely renovated and made fully operational the Blenheim gun turret described above, as well as carrying out many other important tasks on the restoration. He has become an excellent aircraft refinisher and amongst many other immaculate jobs he refurbished and repainted the IWM's P51 Mustang *Big Beautiful Doll* which now has pride of place at Lambeth. Possessed of a dryly wicked sense of humour that has surprised quite a few people with its unerring accuracy, Billy is very popular with the team and excellent company — especially in the pub after work!

A great loss to the Blenheim team was the sudden death of 'Chalky' White early in 1985, when he went into hospital with what started as a minor eye infection. A Welshman christened Edgar, though forever 'Chalky', he was a retired fully-licensed engine man whose great depth of knowledge and experience on early aircraft piston engines was absolutely invaluable. Working

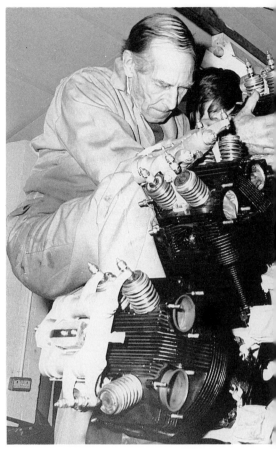

Above left *Billy Kelly working on the complicated hydraulic mechanism of the turret. He restored this to operational condition virtually single-handed.*

Above right *Edgar White, universally known as Chalky, was a craftsman of the old school. Here he is mounting a reconditioned cylinder with assistance from John Romain.*

part-time on the beautifully made Bristol engines with the Blenheim team at Duxford gave him a new lease of life, and an interest and sense of purpose that he had found lacking in retirement. His favourite song was *It's a great big shame*, but he only knew the chorus not the verse and would sing it morning noon and night!

'Chalky' stripped the pile of seized Mercury engines right down, revelling in the high standards of manufacture that they revealed, and he communicated his great enthusiasm and understanding of old engines to the whole team. He would heave them about the engine shop in a way which was amazing for such a small, wiry man. He spent many months honing pistons into barrels, matching and balancing them perfectly; he ground in valves and would leave the barrels inverted for days with the valves closed and petrol inside to make sure none leaked through any imperfect seal; he made a fuel-flow rig for the carburettors to check that they were absolutely spot-on. His workmanship was meticulous.

Most fortunately he passed on much of his unrivalled knowledge and expertise to John Romain, for as he carefully built-up one engine on its stand he explained it all to John and later supervised in detail while John was building up the other one alongside. Young John proved an apt and receptive trainee, so in a sense 'Chalky' is still with the team. We all knew he was delighted when the engines fired up straight away and ran perfectly after their rebuilds, even though he was not present physically. We were glad, in a way, that he did not live to see the loss of the aircraft and his beloved engines, for it would have broken his heart.

Chalky was introduced by Fred Hanson, the original highly experienced engineer supervising the project, who has been a great help throughout the restoration and who too has passed on a fund of information and expertise. Fred supervises the team that looks after the Boeing B17 'Flying Fortress' *Sally B* at Duxford as Chief Engineer so was — and indeed still is — a frequent visitor to Duxford and thus able to keep a fatherly eye on the Blenheim restoration. His advice was always sensible and sound from an aeronautical engineering point of view, and although frequently expressed in a gloriously pithy, down-to-earth manner, it was invariably invaluable.

Norman Chapman, a mutual friend of Fred and 'Chalky', is another really wonderful engineer of the old school who has been of enormous practical assistance to the Blenheim restoration. Always cheerful and smiling, whatever the problems or pressures, Norman is ever helpful; he now looks after Robs Lamplough's aircraft collection at North Weald. During the war he worked on Blenheims for 139 Squadron as a fitter, from the first sortie on 3 September 1939 on, and was with them in France throughout the German advance to Dunkirk.

The wealth of experience and knowledge held in those three heads and in those three pairs of hands is incomparable. Indeed anything about old aeroplanes that was not known by those three between them just wasn't worth knowing!

Many and diverse are the characters who have worked on the Blenheim team: Bob Hewitt, a gruff lorry-driver from Yorkshire whose fruity language we southerners found hard to understand, but who put in a lot of hard work in the early stages; Nick Goodwyn who started with us as a lad and who has now passed out from the RAF College at Cranwell and is piloting fast-jets; Bob Sparkes a very sound design draftsman who has progressed well from Marshalls at Cambridge Airfield to BAe at Hatfield, and who is still working steadily on the second restoration. His ability to produce proper engineering drawings is sometimes very useful.

Christian Hollyer is an aircraft electrical engineer with Qualitair, now at Coventry, whose humour is even more acerbic than Bill's, and whose verbal duels with 'Smudge' were punningly funny; Neville Gardner who started helping with the first restoration while still a lanky young apprentice at RAF

The team unusually smart for the visit of HM The Queen Mother. Robert Sparkes, Hugh Smith, Roy Pullan, John Romain, John Smith, Colin Swann, Christian Hollyer and David Swann.

Another shot of the Blenheim team in front of their creation: Colin Swann, Chief Pilot John 'Larks' Larcombe, Graham Warner, Chief Engineer and pilot John Romain, Christian Hollyer, John 'Smudge' Smith, Billy Kelly, John Gullick, Bob Sparkes, and Nick Goodwyn — only Dave Swann and Hugh Smith were absent.

Halton (therefore another ex 'brat') is now a 6ft 2in RAF sergeant working on Phantoms during the weeks and on Blenheim engines at the weekend, sometimes with the aid of his father Cliff, a BAe engineer; Mike Terry is a keen and hard-working young man, who is full-time at Duxford and works on other BAM aircraft such as the Lysander as well as the Blenheim, but has put in most of his hours on the latter.

Two of the pilots, not a breed noted for getting their hands dirty, have also made a great contribution to the Blenheim restoration: Roy Pullan, being a skilful woodworker, made a very good job of fabricating the wooden bomb-doors and the moulds for the cockpit glazing (as will be described later); and John Larcombe was particularly helpful, mainly behind the scenes in locating hard-to-find materials, as well as test flying the Blenheim and several of our other ex-military aircraft.

Working mainly on these other aircraft too are Ian Arnold, Malcolm Chapman and Barry 'Knuckles' Wright, three excellent team members who, with Billy, are currently making a beautiful job of rebuilding a Harvard, but they lend a hand on the Blenheim too as needed. We also have a good 'apprentice' in young James Gilmour, who is still at school; you will hear later how his father Andy is helping the team.

Viewed as individuals they represent a collection of widely disparate shapes, sizes, ages, jobs and personalities; but viewed together they are united into a cheerfully homogeneous and close-knit team by their shared dedication to making a Blenheim take to the skies again.

Despite being completely shattered by the loss of their lovingly restored Blenheim within weeks of completion, the Blenheim into which they had put so much personal effort and work over so many years, they are now working away on the second rebuild with just as much, if not more, of the enthusiasm and cheerful determination that they displayed on the first.

Judged on their great achievements so far they are demonstrably the best team at Duxford and many believe them to be the best team in the whole aircraft restoration movement. I am glad and proud fully to share that belief.

Chapter Six

The Blenheim in the Second World War

It will help readers to understand the actual restoration process better if a brief description is given of the genesis, design and construction of the Bristol Blenheim, setting it in the context of its period. Further, it will help readers to share our conviction as to the historic importance of the Blenheim if some of its illustrious history is indicated. This history is of necessity only highlighted briefly, for to do it proper justice would require a volume many times larger than this!

For its day, the mid-1930s, the Bristol Blenheim was a highly advanced alloy monocoque design — 'absolute state-of-the-art technology' as we now would say — although it was not originally designed as a bomber.

The Bristol Type 135 was first shown at the 1934 Paris Salon as an intended light, fast six-seat, passenger-aircraft with two 500 hp Bristol Aquila radial engines. It aroused the keen interest of Lord Rothermere, then proprietor of the *Daily Mail*. He had been Britain's first Secretary of State for Air in 1918 and actively encouraged aviation matters. He wanted 'the fastest commercial aircraft in Europe' and wished to demonstrate that the British aircraft industry could produce such a machine, so he personally commissioned an improved version of the aircraft.

The Bristol Aircraft Company, although concerned lest they should upset their best customer the Air Ministry, responded with the Bristol Type 142, re-engined with 640 hp Bristol Mercury engines, slightly enlarged to eight seats, and given the greater range that he had specified.

As a great patriot Lord Rothermere named it with pride *Britain First*. He had an eye on his main business rival Lord Beaverbrook, owner of the *Daily Express*, who had just ordered a Lockheed 12, a similar but far slower American aircraft. Ironically, when Lord Beaverbrook became Minister of Aircraft Production under Churchill in the dark days of 1940, one of the five types he ordered into 'super priority production' was the Bristol Blenheim.

Following early flight tests it was clear that *Britain First* was a quite outstanding high-speed executive aircraft. The Air Ministry sat up and took notice so Lord Rothermere in a most generous and patriotic act presented it to them 'for the nation'. He was not to know that in a few years' time many brave crews would indeed selflessly put 'Britain first' in their devotion to duty, often at the cost of their own lives.

The Bristol 142's potential as a fast, light bomber was most ably demonstrated when on test from RAF Martlesham Heath in 1935, the then sensational top speed of 307 mph (490 km/h) when fully laden proved to be some 60 mph (96 km/h) faster than the Hawker Fury and the Gloster Gauntlet, the RAF's standard biplane single-seat fighters, and 50 mph (80 km/h) faster than the Gloster Gladiator which had only just been ordered as the RAF's new front-line fighter!

The Bristol design team led by Frank Barnwell quickly developed the Type 142 *Britain First* into the Type 142M (for military) by raising the wing from a low to a central position to provide an enclosed bomb-bay, deleting the cabin windows and reconfiguring the nose to accommodate (just) a navigator/bomb-aimer to the right of the pilot, strengthening the structure, and adding a semi-retractable dorsal-turret, a wing-mounted, forward-firing gun and other military equipment.

The RAF, at the nadir of its between-the-wars state of chronic under-equipment, immediately ordered it in large numbers 'straight off the drawing board' as an overdue step in a rapid expansion programme. The aircraft was named Blenheim after the estate given by Queen Anne on behalf of the grateful nation to John Churchill, First Duke of Marlborough, after his great victory

Bristol Type 142 'Britain First', which first flew on 12 April 1935, soon creating a sensation with its speed. Commissioned by Lord Rothermere, it was presented by him to the nation in a generous and patriotic gesture, and led directly to the Blenheim.

Top *Bristol Type 142M (for Military) prototype Blenheim, K7033, which made its initial flight on 25 June 1936. It was the first of over 6,000 Blenheims which were produced over the next six years up to June 1943.*

Above *Early production Blenheim Mk I. This aircraft, K7037, was one of over 100 lost in accidents prior to the outbreak of war: it crashed on take-off at Wyton on 10 May 1938.*

over the French in 1704 at the small Bavarian village of Blenheim.

The prototype Blenheim Mark I was tested by the RAF in 1936 when the additional weight and drag of the military equipment had already reduced the top speed to 281 mph (450 km/h), over 25 mph (40 km/h) slower than *Britain First*, despite the substitution of 850 hp Mercury VIIIs for the 640 hp Mercury VIs. Most of the extra drag came from the power-operated dorsal gun-turret, even though it was made semi-retractable by an ingenious but for the period complicated hydraulic mechanism. Bear in mind that in contemporary aircraft the rear gunner stood up in an open cockpit with his single machine-gun on a metal ring mounting.

When in squadron service Blenheims rarely exceeded 265 mph (424 km/h) as more equipment and armour was added, and the drag of matt camouflage paint was higher than the polished alloy of *Britain First*. The all-up weight increased continually from under 9,000 lb (4,082 kg) to 14,500 lb (6,576 kg) for a fully laden wartime Blenheim, and this of course adversely affected the performance. But in pre-war exercises Blenheims still successfully out-ran or evaded fighters and greatly impressed both service chiefs and the pilots who flew them — or were unable to catch them in their fighters.

However, aircraft designers were about to produce much more advanced monoplane fighters — the Hurricane and Spitfire in Great Britain, and, far more ominously, the Messerschmitt Bf 109 in Germany — with expected speeds of some 325 to 350 mph (520 to 560 km/h). Although both the Royal Air Force and the new Luftwaffe subscribed to the then prevelent theory that 'the bomber would always get through', the writing was already on the wall.

Once the 'shooting war' really started in May 1940, the fallacy of the theory was demonstrated at great cost by the very heavy losses incurred by RAF bombers of all types during daylight operations, as well as by Luftwaffe bombers to the RAF fighters in the Battle of Britain. Both Air Forces were soon forced to resort to far less accurate night bombing, for which both were equally unprepared.

Crews coming straight from Hawker Hinds, Demons or other unsophistica-ted fixed-undercarriage biplanes found the Blenheim very fast and complicated, for it was definately a 'hot ship' in its day, and there were quite a lot of flying accidents. This situation was compounded by the lack of proper conversion training as later adopted, the absence of check-lists of cockpit drills and vital actions, and complete ignorance of single-engined flying techniques in twin-engined aircraft.

The crews needed to acclimatize themselves to the much higher levels of performance, to learn the correct use of such new devices as powerful flaps and wheel brakes, retractable undercarriages, and variable-pitch props (all with ergonomically poor control layouts), together with complicated engine handling of the powerful supercharged engines.

On the Blenheim some of the vital controls, such as the push-pull plungers which changed the propeller pitch, were behind the pilot's left elbow above a pair of identical plungers which operated the carburettor cut-off controls, although these were later protected by a sprung-loaded flap. Each pair was painted red for the port (left) engine and green for the starboard (right) engine. So closing down the correct engine in a hurry whilst struggling to maintain control of the aircraft following, for example, engine trouble soon after take-off at night was fraught with difficulties. As one ex-Blenheim pilot said, 'You needed a colour-sensitive left elbow which could see in the dark and act bloody quickly.'

Woe betide the pilot who failed to warm up his engines sufficiently, or who neglected to 'clear the plugs' before take-off, or who opened the throttles too suddenly and got a 'rich cut', or who attempted to take off in course pitch or weak mixture. These and similar mistakes were frequent and often fatal. Over

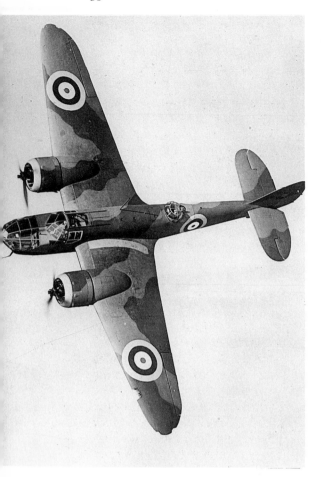

100 Blenheims, nearly 10 per cent of the total deployed, had been lost through flying accidents prior to the outbreak of war.

The Blenheim 'Short Nose' Mark I also suffered from a very cramped crew position for the observer/navigator, who found it difficult even to open a map, and was fairly short on range too. Various versions of an extended nose to provide a proper navigation table and seat, with a bomb-aiming window, were tried, but they all restricted the pilot's view too much, especially on take-off and landing. Finally the port side of the extended glazed nose was scalloped down above the navigation table to give the characteristic asymmetric nose shape of the Mark IV 'Long Nose' Blenheim, and at the same time the long-range outer wing tanks were fitted, plus some other modifications.

This improved Mk IV version (Mks II and III were not proceeded with) was the Bristol Type 149, but production carried on throughout 1938 and 1939 under the same Air Ministry contracts and on the same Bristol and Avro production lines as the Type 142 Mark Is. Indeed many Blenheims on the line that started production as Mk Is were finished as Mk IVs.

The Rootes 'shadow factory' at Speke later produced more Mk IVs than Bristols and Avro put together. The Type 149 Mk IV was also built under licence in Canada from 1939, Bristols sending out four complete Mark IVs as patterns, plus all the drawings and jigs, as well as complete power plants. They were also licence-built in Finland and Yugoslavia.

The last version to be introduced was the Type 160 Mark V, initially known as the Bisley, which was produced right up to mid-1943, although by then it was clearly obsolescent. But extra armour and armament put the weight up to over 17,000 lb (7,708 kg) — more than double the empty weight of a Mk I. Even with the 950 hp Mercury 30s and constant-speed propellers they were slower and even more vulnerable than the Mark IV and very unpopular with their crews, ending the Blenheims' illustrious wartime service on a sad and somewhat sour note.

Apart from being the first all-metal, stressed-skin, cantilever monoplane with retractable undercarriage, flaps and variable-pitch propellers ever ordered for the RAF — and in unprecedented numbers too — the Blenheim achieved many other notable 'firsts' during its long career.

The very first sortie of the Second World War was a reconnaissance of the German fleet off Wilhelmshaven by a Blenheim IV of 139 Squadron which took of at 12:02 hrs on 3 September 1939, while Chamberlain was still telling the nation that 'a state of war exists between this country and Germany'. F/O McPhearson found the German capital ships but his Blenheim's radio failed and its camera froze up, so the attacking force of Blenheims standing by could not be sent that day.

The following day the attack was mounted as the first offensive sortie of the war: 15 Blenheims took off, five failed to find the German fleet in the poor weather and returned with their bombs still on board. Of the 10 that attacked, five were shot down by anti-aircraft fire. The few bombs that did score hits on the battleship *Admiral Scheer* did little damage, mainly bouncing off the German armour-plating — indeed the most damage was caused by the Blenheim crashing into the cruiser *Emden*. Sadly this raid was a portent of the many bravely executed but largely ineffective Blenheim raids that were to follow.

Blenheims were the first aircraft fitted with then revolutionary air-to-air radar, becoming the RAF's first dedicated night fighters, and one scored the world's first successful radar interception and shot down a Dornier 17 on the night of 2 July 1940. The service's first dedicated PR (photograhic reconnaissance) aircraft was also a Blenheim 'cleaned up' at Heston in 1939.

The fighter version of the Blenheim, with a belly-mounted pack of four machine-guns, made the first RAF attack on the German mainland when they straffed the seaplane base at Borkum on 28 November 1939. Blenheims made the first reconnaissance sorties to the Ruhr by day and night, and the first night-intruder attacks on German airfields. Night fighter Blenheims served throughout the blitz on London and other British cities until they were replaced by their more effective young brothers, Bristol Beaufighters.

The first aircraft to sink a German U-boat was a Blenheim, on 11 March

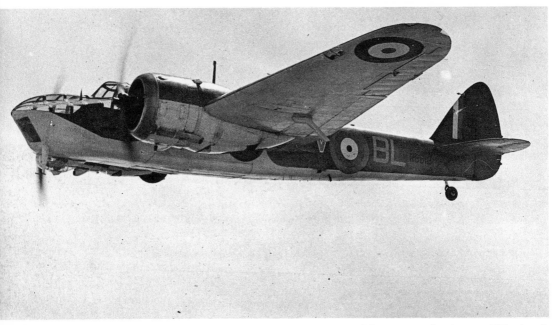

A 1940 photo of V Victor of 40 Squadron — note the rear-defence gun under the nose. This aircraft, R3612, was lost on 9 September 1940 attacking invasion barges at Ostend.

1940, as was the first aircraft to sink a Japanese submarine, on 23 February 1942, as well as the first Japanese submarine to be sunk by an RCAF aircraft, on 7 July 1942.

Seven squadrons of Mk IV F's were in Fighter Command during the Battle of Britain and played a significant part when they broke up a strong German daylight raid on the north-east coast, shooting down several bombers from Luftflotte 5 in Norway (who could not be escorted by Bf 109s as the range of the fighters was insufficient), thus discouraging any further such attacks and enabling Dowding to concentrate his single-seat fighters in the south-east.

Dangerous low-level daylight attacks on enemy shipping by many Blenheim squadrons of both Coastal Command and 2 Group, Bomber Command, were almost continuous, but at a high cost in casualties. During the Battle of Britain Bomber Command lost far more aircrew than Fighter Command.

Early on 17 May, 12 Blenheims of 82 Squadron set out on a daylight raid against a Panzer column near Gembloux; only one returned — on one engine — and that was damaged beyond repair. The entire squadron had been wiped out, but was immediately reformed by the CO the Earl of Bandon (known as Paddy) and was in action again on 20 May. On 13 August another 12 Blenheims of 82 Squadron set out to attack the German-held airfield at Aarborg in Northern Denmark; all 11 aircraft that reached the target were shot down.

Aarborg was but one of over 70 German-occupied airfields that were attacked by 2 Group Blenheims. Many enemy ports were raided too, including the

A Blenheim Mk IV of 105 Squadron taxying to dispersal on a wartime grass airfield — actually our restored aircraft, accurately marked as V6028 GB-D.

daring daylight attack on Bremen lead by 'Hughie' Edwards that resulted in the award of the Victoria Cross. The first deep-penetration daylight raid into Germany was carried out by a force of 54 Blenheims, unescorted beyond the Dutch coast, on the power stations at Cologne on 12 August 1941. Blenheims were used as bait for the German fighters in the heavily escorted 'Circus' operations.

Blenheims carried out the first attack on the Italians when they joined the war on the German side, striking El Adem airfield on 11 May 1940. They fought in Greece and in the Western Desert, they hampered Rommel's supplies from bases in Malta. On 4 December 1942 nine Blenheims sent to attack a German airfield near Tunis were all shot down. Their leader Wing Commander Hugh Malcolm was awarded a posthumous VC.

They fought against the Japanese in Burma, Singapore, Malaya, India and Sumatra. Squadron Leader Scarff had been the sole survivor from an attacking force of Blenheims in December 1941, and carried out his attack single-handed; he crash-landed back at base but died of his injuries within hours, and he too was posthumously awarded the VC. These are but examples of the countless acts of heroism, often unrecorded, carried out by the brave 'Blenheim Boys'.

Blenheims were in the thick of the fighting from Norway to Sicily, mainly by day but often by night. So much for the man who said to me at Duxford, 'They didn't do much in the war, did they?'

All agreed that the earlier Blenheims were superb machines to fly, but they were just not fast enough to escape the more modern interceptors they came up against. The rapid development of heavily armed, single-seater fighters with far superior performance had overtaken the Blenheims.

For example, the Bf 109 was not only considerably faster but with its 20 mm cannon armament could also keep out the range of the single (later twin) rifle-bore .303 in 'pea-shooter' machine-guns which were the only rear defence for the Blenheims, and shoot them down with virtual immunity. The Blenheim gunner may have sat in a powered turret, but his fire-power had not improved over his First World War compatriot standing in an open cockpit!

Several Blenheim Squadrons tried fitting rear-firing machine-guns in the back of the fuselage, or in the rear of the engine nacelles, but they were useless. An under-nose blister with one (later two) rearward-firing gun was also fitted to many Blenheims, aimed by the observer through mirrors, but it was equally useless and only added to the drag and weight, thus reducing performance even further.

So the Blenheims lacked sufficient performance to escape attack and were under-armed and poorly protected when they were caught, and thus unable to defend themselves adequately, so ended up with the worst of both worlds. German anti-aircraft defences too, both light and medium, were far more effective and widespread than expected, especially in the instant deployment of mobile multiple 20 mm and 37 mm cannon units, backed by the excellent 88 mm anti-tank and anti-aircraft guns, by the advancing Panzer armoured formations. They also exacted a grave toll from the lightly armoured, low-flying Blenheims. What had been the last word in modernity in 1936 was so rapidly overtaken by the German introduction of faster, better-armed fighters and deadly efficient AA fire that even by 1940 they were exposed to risks that were verging on the unacceptable, and the losses throughout 1941 and 1942 mounted inexorably.

During the battle for France, some 200 Blenheims had been lost in a few weeks. This had been anticipated by and so deeply concerned the then Air Officer Commanding Bomber Command, Charles Portal (later Lord Portal, Chief of the Air Staff), that early in May 1940, worried at the losses of his highly skilled Blenheim crews, he had written to the Air Staff: 'I am convinced that the proposed use of these Blenheim units is fundamentally unsound, and that if it is persisted in, it is likely to have disastrous consequences on the future of the war in the air.'

This letter was parallel to the famous plea of his equivalent Hugh Dowding, the AOC Fighter Command, direct to Churchill not to send any more of his precious Fighter Squadrons to France, and equally prescient.

But the Blenheims, despite their obvious shortcomings, just had to be pressed into constant action, however high the risks and losses, for they were by far the most numerous offensive aircraft, indeed often the only aircraft for daylight offensive operations, that the RAF had available at the time. The Blenheim squadrons and their brave crews suffered accordingly.

I believe that I have demonstrated that the heavy losses incurred were not because the Blenheim itself was a bad aircraft — indeed it was a fine aircraft to fly, and it often absorbed severe damage and still flew home — but because it was our main means at that stage of the war of carrying the war back to the enemy, an enemy who, with German thoroughness, had developed their own defensive capabilities both rapidly and effectively.

I hope that this brief mention of some of their achievements will enable you to re-appraise the significance of the many contributions to the war effort made by those gallant crews in their Bristol Blenheims. Also you may now acknowledge more readily than before the very great but hitherto understated importance of the Blenheim to the history of the Royal Air Force during the war. I trust that you will agree that the restoration of a Blenheim to flying condition was not only overdue but also certainly well worth while.

Some important Blenheim 'firsts'	
FIRST all-metal cantilever monoplane of stressed-skin construction with retractable undercarriage, flaps and variable-pitch propellors ordered for the RAF.	August 1935
FIRST delivery to 114 Sqn RAF at Wyton (who operated them for 6 years).	17/3/1937
FIRST aircraft in the world equipped with air-to-air radar; 25 Sqn RAF had 15 Mk 1F aircraft with AI Mk 1 fitted.	August 1939
FIRST aircraft to reach 1,000 deliveries under pre-war RAF expansion scheme: 1,089 — more than any other type — were on charge at the outbreak of war.	3/9/1939
FIRST sortie of World War II, Mk IV N6215 of 139 Sqn, 1202 hours.	3/9/1939
FIRST bombing raid of World War II, attack on German Fleet off Wilhelmshaven.	4/9/1939
FIRST attack on German mainland, Borkum.	28/11/1939
FIRST decorations of World War II: DFCs to Blenheim pilots Flt/Lt Doran of 110 Sqn and F/O McPhearson of 139 Sqn. Wyton	11/1939
FIRST dedicated RAF Night Fighter, Blenheim Mk 1F.	late 1939
FIRST dedicated RAF Photo Recce aircraft, Blenheim L1348, Heston.	late 1939
FIRST Night Intruder sorties against enemy airfields.	21/12/1939
FIRST RAF aircraft to sink a U-Boat (U31), Blenheim IV P4852 of 82 Sqn.	11/3/1940
FIRST aircraft with centimetric radar in nose-dome, Blenheim V4888.	early 1940
FIRST RAF sortie of World War II against Italy.	11/5/1940
FIRST ever successful interception using air-to-air radar (AI Mk3).	2/7/1940
FIRST deep-penetration unescorted low-level daylight raid, Cologne power stations.	12/8/1941
FIRST 'Combined Operation' with Navy and Army, South Vaagso, Norway.	28/12/1941
Also Dieppe 'Combined Operation'.	19/8/1942
FIRST RAF aircraft to sink a Japanese submarine, Mk IV of 84 Sqn.	23/2/1942
FIRST RCAF aircraft to sink a Japanese submarine, Mk IV of 155 Sqn.	7/7/1942
FIRST and ONLY RAF aircraft to serve in every wartime RAF Command (Fighter, Bomber, Coastal, Army Co-operation and Training Commands) and in every Theatre of War.	

Chapter Seven

Nuts and bolts

L et me now describe the actual layout and method of construction of the
Blenheim with a brief semi-technical description, for this will help you to
appreciate better the actual process of completely restoring the aircraft.
This description is of necessity a little technical, although perhaps not sufficiently so for the aviation expert. I have tried to strike a happy balance, but
completely non-technical readers will be excused if they skip this chapter!

The Blenheim is an all-metal, mainly alloy, stressed-skin monocoque tail-
wheel monoplane with a cantilver mid-wing, and a single fin and rudder. It is
powered by two Bristol 'Mercury' air-cooled radial piston engines mounted
centrally on either end of a straight wing centre section, with detachable outer
wings set at the required dihedral angle. The entire aircraft is alloy-covered,
apart from the control surfaces which are covered in fabric.

A retractable main undercarriage is fitted, with twin suspension oleos for each
12 in alloy mainwheel, retracting rearwards, and incorporating a wheel-bay
fairing which leaves part of the retracted wheel exposed as was the fashion in
those days. This lessened the damage if the aircraft was landed, either
inadvertently or deliberately in the case of a forced landing, with the wheels still
retracted!

Large split-trailing-edge flaps run the full span of the wings inboard from the
Frise-type ailerons to the fuselage. They are in two sections, divided by the
wing-joints just outboard of the engine nacelles and retract flush into recesses
beneath the wings; both these flaps and the undercarriage are hydraulically
operated. The drum brakes on the main wheels are pneumatically operated.

The engines are closely cowled with baffles between the cylinders, and both
inner and outer cowlings to regulate the airflow through controllable annular
cooling grills set at the rear of the detachable outer cowlings and in front of the
upper and lower streamlined engine nacelles. The engines have crankshaft-

driven centrifugal superchargers, and drive de Havilland two-position, variable pitch (but non-feathering), three-bladed metal propellors via epicyclic reduction gears on the front of the crankshaft.

Most fortunately for the restoration team the construction of the Blenheim utilized various alloys throughout, apart from tubular steel engine and undercarriage mounting bays and parts of the front and rear wing main spars.

These spars are fabricated from alloy vertical webs, reinforced by vertical stringers, with high-tensile steel upper and lower angled booms which act as the main stiffeners, further supported for most of the span by curved steel cornices. More will be heard of these steel sections later, as they contained the most serious areas of corrosion that we discovered on the whole airframe. The rest of the alloy structure was relatively corrosion free and had withstood its 40 years' exposure to the rigours of harsh Canadian winters remarkably well.

The all-alloy fuselage is made in three main demountable parts; nose and rear fuselage sections, plus the stern frame. The nose section includes the cockpit back to just aft of the front wing spar. The cockpit has a large transparent sliding-hatch above it, and an emergency hatch below the nose. It is built of several full or part frames with flanged stringers and stiffeners, all alloy-covered apart from the transparent sections which are mounted on shaped alloy tubes. The pilot's seat chassis is a separate structure, and the floor of mixed wood and alloy construction.

The rear fuselage section fits over the aft part of the wing centre section and mates with the nose section (both being strengthened by a central vertical alloy keel-plate beneath the wing, which divides the bomb-bay lengthways). It incorporates the semi-retractable, hydraulically power-operated dorsal gun-turret and upper and lower exit hatches. The rear section comprises the strong stern frame, which supports the fin post (on to which the rudder is hinged), the tailplane spar mountings, and the tailwheel mounting.

All three fuselage sections comprise a series of shaped alloy channel-section transverse formers, with flanged stiffeners and lengthways stringers, and an Alclad dural stressed-skin covering, all riveted together. The transport joints between all three sections are further strengthened by alloy butt-straps.

The immensely strong wing centre section is the core of the whole aircraft and absorbs all the major loads. The engines, main undercarriage, outer wings, main fuel tanks, the nose and rear fuselage sections, and in wartime the bomb-load, are all carried directly by this centre section.

This centre section is, as mentioned above, straight, tapering outwards only in chord and depth, with two full-depth parallel spars linked by alloy ribs and spanwise stringers, with a central well between the spars, the floor of which forms the roof of the bomb-bay and is strengthened accordingly, all with a stressed-skin covering in dural. The lower surface is almost flat, with most of the taper on the upper surface, and the dihedral of 6° 30′ (the angle the wings tilt upwards to assist lateral stability) is all on the outer wings. This gives the Blenheim its characteristic, slightly gull-winged, appearance when viewed head-on.

The inner flaps retract flush under the trailing edge of the centre section; all the engine and flying controls, plus the fuel and hydraulic lines and selector controls, etc, are mounted on the front of the main-spar, covered by the leading edge which fastens to D-shaped formers bolted to the spar. The main fuel tanks, made in aluminium, are mounted on special formers in a bay between the spars inboard of the undercarriage bays. These latter bays are strong cross-braced tubular steel structures bolted between the spars, with the circular engine mountings, also of braced tubular steel construction and incorporating a fire-resistant bulkhead, bolted on to the front.

The outer wings are of similar construction to the centre section, with the two main spars (fabricated by the same alloy web and steel boom method as the centre section spars) tapering off towards the tips, and alloy flanged ribs with lipped lightening holes, and span-wise flanged stringers, all clad with a dural stressed-skin. The wings are fastened to the ends of the centre section spars via special cross-bolted lug attachments on the corresponding outer-wing spars.

The aileron controls pass via a system of push-pull rods and cranks from the front to the rear of the wing; the arms of the outer cranks are of different lengths to give the ailerons their differential operation. There is provision for an outer fuel tank in each wing, immediately outboard of the engines, but we did not use these. The outer flaps fit under the trailing edge outboard to the ailerons, which are also of alloy construction on a tubular spar, but covered in fabric not alloy. The port wing has a landing lamp behind a Perspex fairing in the outer leading edge. The curved formers for the wing-tips are shaped in wood with an alloy covering, and contain white formation lamps and red (port) and green (starboard) wing-tip lights.

The tail assembly is built in the same alloy stressed-skin manner, with three transverse alloy frames in the stern frame, the fourth and main frame being made of steel as it carries the loads from the tailplane spars via their attachments, as well as the loads from the fin and rudder via the box-section fin-post. This extends the full height from the bottom of the fuselage to the top of the fin, and is bolted to the rear of the stern frame, which also carried the loads from the tail-wheel mounted on the curved lower portion. The control cables operate the elevators, rudder and trim-tabs through cross shafts which pivot on the same frame.

The one-piece cantilever tailplane has twin spars, smaller versions of the wing spars, with flanged alloy ribs, stringers and stiffeners, and is alloy covered. The two elevators are of similar alloy construction but based on a tubular spar, have adjustable trimming tabs, curved wooden formers at the tips, and are fabric-covered. The large rudder is of matching construction and also has an adjustable trim-tab, plus navigation and formation lights. All the control surfaces incorporate both static and aerodynamic balancing.

The Bristol Mercury engines are nine cylinder, single-row, air-cooled radials, of 24.9 litres capacity (ie each cylinder at 2.76 litres is larger than most car engines!) and develop a maximum of 950 bhp at 2,350 rpm. They were a supercharged development of the 'Jupiter' radial which had its origins in the First World War. Mercury engines were used on the Gladiator, Gauntlet, Bulldog, Lysander, Master, etc, as well as on the Blenheim.

The Bristol Pegasus, used on the Swordfish, Wellesley, Bombay, Walrus, Hampden, Wellington, etc, was an enlarged (28.7 litres) version of the Mercury with the same bore of 146 cm but a stroke of 190.5 cm, as opposed to the 165 cm of the Mercury, and developed 980 bhp. Later and much more powerful Bristol engines, the very successful Hercules and Centaurus ranges, were two-row radials and had sleeve valves. These had fewer moving parts which gave smoother operation and higher rpm, and although larger in capacity the overall diameter was reduced which lessened drag considerably. They powered such aircraft as the Beaufighter, Halifax and Stirling throughout the war and such aircraft as the Sea Fury, Brigand and Hastings after the war until the advent of gas turbine engines.

Not many people realize that during the war Bristols manufactured more of their air-cooled radial aircraft engines than Rolls-Royce did of their liquid-cooled V12s. When you think of the vast number of Merlin-powered Lancasters, Mosquitoes, Spitfires, Hurricanes, etc, this is a surprising fact.

The Mercury engines are built up on an alloy split-crankcase with finned steel cylinder barrels, screwed and shrunk into heavily finned alloy cylinder heads. These contain hemispherical combustion chambers each with four overhead poppet valves, operated by external push-rods and rocker arms with adjustable tappets. Each combustion chamber has two spark-plugs fired from dual shaft-driven BTH or Rotax magnetos, which have a variable timing device interconnected to the carburettors to give the best ignition setting for various throttle openings. The sodium-filled exhaust valves are to the better-cooled front of the engine, and the 18 tubular exhaust manifolds discharge into an annular stainless steel exhaust collector ring which forms the leading edge of the close-fitting engine cowling.

Clutch-driven from the rear of the crankshaft, the single-stage centrifugal compressor delivers the mixture via a circular volute casing with diffuser vanes, from a Claudel-Hobson carburettor, tangentially via the 18 inlet manifolds to the inlet valves at the rear of the cylinder heads at a pressure of up to plus 9 psi of boost. The boost pressure and mixture are maintained automatically by the very involved Claudel-Hobson carburettors at the settings selected by the pilot irrespective of altitude or engine speed. The twin-choke updraught multi-jet carburettors have powerful accelerator pumps, one with a 1.5 second delayed action, to richen the mixture by injecting neat fuel as the throttles are opened, to cater for the increased fuel demand of an accelerating engine. It follows that the throttles must be opened carefully, smoothly and progressively as is made clear in the Pilot's Notes, three seconds being given as the optimum time.

The short-skirt alloy pistons have lightly domed crowns and three compression and two oil-control piston rings each. The very stiff and short forged crank-shaft is fully machined with an integral master connecting rod, and eight articulated connecting rods, and is splined on the front to receive the propeller reduction gears and on the rear to drive the clutches for the supercharger impellor. The two-row camshaft 'drum', driven by gears which incorporate a vernier adjustment for timing, runs concentric to the crankshaft at one-eighth engine speed and in the reverse direction! Each row operates the exhaust or inlet pushrods via roller tappets and a rocker system with a device to compensate for expansion and maintain the tappet clearances as adjusted.

The engines are pressure lubricated on the dry-sump principle with a remote oil reservoir mounted on top of the undercarriage bay in each upper rear nacelle. Hot engine oil is pumped through special chambers in the carburettors adjacent to the chokes to help prevent carburettor icing, which was a major problem on piston engines of this era. There are engine-driven, combined oil-pressure and oil-scavenge pumps, with oil-cleaners and ducted cylindrical oil-coolers; there is also an engine-driven fuel pump, vacuum pump, compressed-air pump and generator.

The propellors are de Havilland, oil-controlled, bracket-type, two-pitch (with 10° movement from course to fine), non-feathering units. The three alloy blades are 11 ft in diameter, and they were a great advance in efficiency on the wooden, fixed-pitch propellers fitted to most contemporary RAF aircraft.

So it can be seen that the Blenheim was highly advanced when designed in the early 1930s, but was overtaken by the rapid improvements in fighter aircraft performance even while it was being mass-produced in the late '30s. Nevertheless it represented a most important if not vital element in the re-equipment of the RAF, just before the war, and certainly more than proved its worth in it. Without the great contributions of the Blenheims, the desperate plight of the RAF and therefore the country in the early 1940s may well have become completely disastrous.

The principal dimensions and performance figures for the Bristol Type 149 Blenheim Mk IV are:

Wingspan 56 ft 4 in (17.17m), *length* 42 ft 9 in (13.03m), *wing area* 469 sq ft (43.57 sq m); *height* (tail-down) 12 ft 9 in (3.89 m); *undercarriage track* 15 ft 6 in (4.72 m); *fuel capacity* 468 imperial gallons (2,128 litres); *range* 1,160 miles (1,866 km) at maximum cruise speed of 225 mph (363 km/h), 1,457 miles (2,344 km) at economical cruise speed of 170 mph (274 km/h); *normal endurance* 8.65 hrs, 10.8 hrs with bomb-bay ferry-tanks; *normal bomb-load* 1,000 lb internally, plus 320 lb externally; *service ceiling* 23,000 ft (7,010 m); *initial rate of climb* 1,480 ft (449 m) per minute; *maximum speed* 266 mph (428 km/h) at 15,000 ft (4,575 m) (at max weight), 288 mph (460 km/h) at lower weight, 230 mph (370 km/h) at sea level; *tare weight* 9,240 to 9,790 lb (4,224 to 4,445 kg) depending on equipment/armament; *normal take-off weight* 14,400 lb (6,538 kg); *maximum (overload) take-off weight* 15,682 lb (7,120 kg).

Chapter Eight

Restoration begins

When I took over the abandoned Blenheim restoration and reassembled the team in 1979, the centre fuselage was mounted on trestles in the workshops at 'Blenheim Palace'. It had been stripped of all internal fittings and equipment, partially paint-stripped, and some damaged skin-panels had been removed. But the project had foundered and there it had just sat with very little likelihood of ever being completed.

However, once it had been decided with the re-formed team to go ahead with a complete rebuild to airworthy status, we had to register the aircraft and apply for a permit to fly which, although many years away, allowed the Civil Aviation Authority to send their surveyors at regular intervals to monitor each stage of the work and check every component or major section as it was 'signed off' by our own licensed engineers. All the work was logged as we went along and the files grew fatter and fatter. Someone said that when they weighed as much as the aircraft it would be ready to fly!

We obtained the special civil registration of G-MKIV, which seemed apposite as the ex-RCAF airframe 10038 was a Mk IV. However, we did not intend it to carry these civil marks as we applied to the CAA for exemption from displaying them, because we had decided to finish the aircraft in the correct colours and markings of a 1942 2 Group RAF Bomber Command Blenheim Mk IV aircraft.

Incidentally, it was intended to refinish the aircraft every few years in a different scheme: we had in mind an all-black night-fighter scheme, the green and grey Coastal Command colours, the light and dark brown desert colours, etc. We also had the drawings of and intended to make the four-gun pack of the Mk IV-F fighter variants. This would have helped to remind people of the many roles that the Blenheim played during the war, and given more variety to its air show appearances.

The stripped-out rear fuselage undergoing repair with the lower skin panels removed; the opening for the wing centre-section is on the right.

The interior of the rear fuselage, repaired and partly re-skinned. This view shows the formers and stringers of the all-alloy monocoque construction. The turret opening is top-centre above the lead-light.

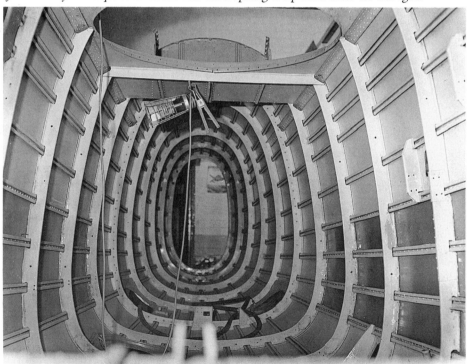

We accumulated copies of both Bristol Aircraft Co and Fairchild Aircraft Co (the original and licensee manufacturers) repair and maintenance manuals and spare parts lists, as well as all the RAF and RCAF manuals and notes on the airframes, engines, carbs and props that we could find — or that were kindly donated to us — and studied them all thoroughly.

The first task on the restoration of the rear or main fuselage, and a long, very messy and laborious one too, was to complete the paint-stripping, both internal and external. This was done entirely by hand using brushed-on liquid stripper, scraping off the partially dissolved paint and working down to the bare metal with more stripper on soft brushes and mildly abrasive pads. When you consider the thousands of awkward corners between the stringers and formers of the internal structure you will understand just what a time-consuming and difficult task this was.

When that job was finally completed, and the whole rear fuselage thoroughly cleaned and de-greased, every single inch of each former, stiffener and stringer was inspected minutely. Any repairs or replacements found necessary were carried out.

Similarly each section of the dural outer skin was examined in detail and then repaired, or a new section of skin made up if the section was beyond repair, and most of the skinning was removed and re-riveted in any case. This was very important as in a monocoque structure the outer skin is stressed to carry most of the loads on the airframe, rather than the formers and stringers which merely hold this outer skin into position and shape. An eggshell is a perfect monocoque, without any formers, and with a very high strength-to-weight ratio!

New sections of flooring were made up for the area of the fuselage around the turret, and forward to the central well between the wing-spars; these floors cover various control and cable runs, etc. We had discovered some old wartime .303 in cartridge cases under the original floor panels! The rear escape-hatch with its built-in camera mounting and window was also rebuilt at this stage. The whole fuselage section was then etch-primed inside and out, section at a time, and the interior painted with a 'cockpit green'.

The fuselage nose section, standing upright on its rear face or sitting the right way up on separate trestles, underwent exactly the same laborious series of treatments; but here there was far more in the way of internal fittings to remove first as it included the cockpit with its mass of equipment, controls, wiring and plumbing.

New floors of marine ply were made up, treated and fitted; similarly the many small wooden panels on the cockpit interior in line with the propellers (to stop fragments of ice thrown off the props from penetrating the thin skin) were renewed and fixed into place.

The pilot's seat, control column and rudder pedals are mounted on a separate tubular chassis and this complete assembly, with all the control runs beneath it, was stripped right down and completely renovated as a separate item, largely by John Gullick. This took many months of patient work, and when it was all completed and painted it was later reinstated into the nose section.

The cockpit and nose framework of light-alloy tubes supporting the alloy

Above left *The lower hatch, constructed mainly of wood, is clamped while the glue sets.*

Left *The pilot's seat and chassis with control column, before rebuilding.*

Above *The cockpit interior being stripped down, showing the rudder pedals (below where the instrument panel used to be) and some of the mass of broken control cables and hydraulic lines.*

glazing bars was stripped down too, carefully reshaped and repaired, for all the glazing had long since gone. Gone too were all the instruments so the main panel for the flight instruments was removed and repaired — we were lucky to buy a complete RAF standard 'blind-flying' panel with all the correct 1940s flight instruments to fit into it — and we fabricated a new panel for the engine and ancillary instruments to the starboard side of the cockpit.

Similarly the central pedestal for engine and trimming controls was removed, stripped, refurbished and re-assembled, as were the controls themselves. Then followed the minor-control pedestal to the left of the pilot's seat and the panels below the main instrument panel into which the rebuilt hydraulic selector controls and secondary instruments and indicators were fitted.

The navigation table, which faces the port side of the nose under the

Above *Work in progress inside the 'gutted' cockpit, in the paint-stripped nose section of the fuselage, which has been stood upright on its rear face for easy access.*

Above right *The interior of the nose, stripped, repaired and primed. The wood inserts can be seen on the left and in the floor, and the compass mounting (left centre) shows where the instrument panel will be.*

scalloped section, was rebuilt and re-instated, complete with its circular seat which was re-covered with the correct green leather. The jettisonable emergency escape hatch beneath this seat was also refurbished and refitted.

The poor observer cannot have been at all comfortable on long sorties, for his other position alongside the pilot was also a small, hard, circular seat. The pilot's seat was a throne in comparison! All the crew had to endure extreme cold and excessive noise, but the observer's work stations were very cramped indeed.

Meanwhile, away from the fuselage, Billy Kelly had taken on the major task of stripping the remains of the complex hydraulically operated gun-turret right down to its many component parts, and then completely refurbishing the entire assembly to a fully operational status. After some three or four years of working quietly away, when he connected the rebuilt turret to a test-rig to supply hydraulic pressure it raised and lowered to its semi-retracted position, and traversed properly from the foot controls, and the gun-mountings elevated and depressed smoothly from the hand controls (with the new leather covered seat lowering as the gun mounting was elevated and vice versa) which pleased him and all of us greatly.

Later we were very lucky to obtain a pair of genuine wartime Browning .303 in machine-guns for it, which we had de-activated, and when they were fitted the whole fully functional turret looked absolutely superb. Naturally Billy laid claim to becoming our first airborne gunner, and 'Smudge' started dieting to be able to get into the turret.

While all this was taking place, the third, stern frame section of the fuselage

Above *The repaired stern section of the fuselage before being fitted to the main fuselage. The pivoting arms for the elevator controls and the tail-wheel mounting can be seen below the empty electrical conduit. The front (oval) frame is alloy, the centre one — on to which the tailplane spar bolts — is steel, and the rear two are alloy. The fin-post bolts on to the rearmost frame.*

Top right *The one-piece tailplane, mounted on a jig, stripped, partially repaired and awaiting re-skinning. The two spars are shown top and bottom, with some repaired stringers between the ribs of the right-hand half.*

Above right *A row of bent alloy propeller blades stripped from their hubs and awaiting repair.*

Right *Typically crowded workshops at 'Blenheim Palace': the main fuselage to the left, tailplanes in the centre foreground, nose section to the right.*

had been stripped right down in another part of the workshops. The tail-wheel assembly, the fin and very dilapidated rudder, and the one-piece tailplane, were each removed for their own separate stripping, inspecting, repairing and rebuilding programmes.

After reducing the stern frame section to its component parts, they were paint-stripped, inspected, repaired and restored in exactly the same way as the nose and centre fuselage sections, finally being etch-primed, re-assembled and painted. We were fortunate in that the main steel former for the stern section had only very mild surface corrosion which was easily treated, for it would have been a difficult item to fabricate.

When the tailplane was stripped down we found that the twin alloy spars, reinforced with laminated steel angles which also attach it to the stern frame, were in remarkably good condition. The all-alloy fin is built up on a box-section trailing edge post which runs down to the bottom of the stern frame to which it is bolted. It too was quite straightforward to rebuild, although the large, double-curved, lower skins which fair the fin into the top of the rear fuselage were difficult.

Various brackets, fittings, control-cable pulleys, mountings, wiring-loom trunking, etc were all individually inspected, repaired or overhauled, and then primed and painted so that they could be put back into place in all three fuselage sections as their individual restorations were completed. As the months stretched into years the painstaking work continued consistently. Progress seemed slow but was sure. We could see a Blenheim gradually but steadily taking shape.

At the same time as this work on the three fuselage sections and their main sub-assemblies was going on in Building 66, work was also underway in the adjacent building, joined by a passage between the stores and the office to the original 'Blenheim Palace'. This other work was initially rebuilding the wing centre section, the largest single piece of the Blenheim structure. This will be described in the next chapter, but when it was sufficiently advanced for wing centre section to be moved out, the adjoining building was turned into an engine-shop.

In the meantime British Aerial Museum had acquired a pair of ex-RCAF Beech 18 'Expediters' that had been left at Prestwick some years earlier by a defunct Canadian Survey Company. One was sold to Anthony Hutton who displays it with the Harvard Formation Team; the other we refurbished and finished in a 1943 US Navy colour scheme, obtained its Certificate of Airworthiness and took to air displays ourselves. This was so that we, as a team, could learn how to operate properly a medium piston-twin in advance of the completion of the Blenheim, not only from the flying training point of view, but also from the ground handling, maintenance and general operational viewpoints.

The Beech 18 was ideal for this purpose as it is like a twin-engined Harvard and served the US Forces as an advanced trainer throughout the war. Being a twin piston-engined, tail-wheel, all-alloy monoplane with retractable under-carriage, variable-pitch props, flaps, etc, and fitted with full dual-controls, it is quite demanding to fly and therefore an excellent training aircraft.

The wing loading and general handling characteristics, both on the ground and in the air, are similar to the Blenheim. Although the power-to-weight ratio and thus the performance is not as good, it provided excellent experience for the team and we still operate it. Indeed in 1989 it was again refurbished and refinished in a 1942 US Army 'Stars and Bars' colour scheme.

As we worked on the airframe over the years we continued to research more thoroughly the history of the Blenheim and its epic service in the RAF. Initially this was to ensure that the restoration was entirely accurate and authentic, but as we came to learn more of just what Blenheims were called upon to do and discovered more of their importance as the RAF's main offensive aircraft in the early years of the war, we became aware of the need to rehabilitate not just the airframe itself but also the very reputation of the Bristol Blenheim.

This was by no means a sudden flash of inspiration but grew into a conviction that gradually but steadily increased as the years went by. We could see that despite its undoubted historic importance this fine aircraft was in danger of becoming the 'forgotten bomber' of the Second World War. So we became ever more determined to put Blenheims and the achievements of their brave crews 'back on the map' and in the public eye at air displays.

As the RAF's Battle of Britain Memorial Flight continues to perpetuate the fame of the Spitfire and Hurricane, and their airworthy Lancaster so effectively reminds the public of the great efforts of Bomber Command, so we were going to put our Blenheim up alongside them for the same purposes. We wanted to make sure that both the Blenheim and their air and ground crews received at last the recognition they so richly deserved.

The team's Beech 18 Expeditor, used as an advanced trainer before operating the Blenheim, as many characteristics were similar.

Chapter Nine

The Blenheim takes shape

In the building adjoining 'Blenheim Palace' and linked to it by a passageway, work had been proceeding all this time and in parallel to the operations already described earlier, on the main centre section of the wing. This is the largest single structure in the aircraft and is very strong indeed as it absorbs all the main loads. It forms the central core of the airframe itself, to which the front and rear fuselage sections, the outer wing panels, and the engine and undercarriage mountings, plus fuel and oil-tanks, and in wartime the bomb-load, are all affixed.

This whole section was mounted on a steel jig by the main spar bolts at the outer ends of the centre section spars, to maintain its shape whilst it too was de-skinned and laboriously paint-stripped, first whilst inverted and then the right way up.

All the flanged ribs, stringers, stiffeners and formers were repaired or replaced as necessary. The wooden strengthening strips beneath the wing walkways were renewed, and the central well surround dismantled and rebuilt, as well as the floor of this well area which forms the roof of the bomb-bay. New firtree section alloy trailing-edge strips were finally located, the same as used on the de Havilland Comet airliner.

Both the front and rear main spars run right through the wing centre section in one length, and they were repaired with new sections in the steel angle pieces that stiffen the alloy webs where slight corrosion had affected them.

The spars were then 'capped' top and bottom, with specially rolled and treated strips of the correct specification steel. These extra new caps were bonded and riveted into place on to the laminated steel angle section booms and these strengthen the spars considerably. The hidden areas beneath the steel cornices that further stiffen the spar-booms were inspected by a remote fibre optic scope, courtesy of KeyMed.

In similar fashion to the angle booms, where any corrosion was found in the curved cornices affected sections were cut out and replaced with lengths of specially shaped and treated spring steel to the rare original specification, a few lengths of which Bristols had found in a remote corner of their stores at Filton. These cornices are not just a simple quarter-circle, for the angle of the shaped booms is not a right-angle, but each is slightly more or less than 90° because the top and bottoms of the spar are not parallel but taper towards the leading edge on the front spar and towards the trailing edge on the rear spar, to suit the curved profile of the wing section. If you imagine a capital I, with the upright stroke representing the vertical web, the upper and lower cross strokes would represent the booms and would be tilted slightly towards each other, and the cornices fit into the corners (see page 116).

We were able to use Bristol Aircraft Company's own approved 'Battle-damage Repair Schemes' from their manual for this demanding work, on both the centre section and the outer wing-panels, to the satisfaction of the CAA, as their surveyors continued to monitor regularly the restoration process.

Meanwhile both the left and right-hand engine and undercarriage-mounting steel sub-assembly structures had been removed from the centre section and stripped right down. All the tubes, the main ones being square section, braced by tubular section ones, plus the mounting brackets, etc, were individually X-rayed and inspected for internal corrosion. They were all subject to a crack-detecting process, treated and repainted. Then these important structural members were re-assembled with all new nuts and bolts prior to bolting them back into their positions between the front and rear spars.

The centre-section (inverted) being repaired, showing the fuel tank bay (with vacuum cleaner!) with the bomb-racks to the right, the inner-flap mounting lower centre, and the undercarriage frame to the left.

The centre-section, the largest part of the structure, being moved from the adjacent workshop into 'Blenheim Palace', after the completion of repairs. The inner flaps and fuel tank bay covers are in position.

The port 'firewall' fabricated in stainless steel, one of our few deviations from standard, with the tubular-steel engine-mounting frame and its circular row of 18 brackets to which the engine is bolted.

The exterior of the rear fuselage, trial mounted on the centre-section. The tailplane is under the cover in the foreground, the turret components on the right.

The rebuilt rudder before being recovered; the slot at the rear is for the trim-tab. The alloy tubes are conduits for the electric cables to the navigation and formation lights.

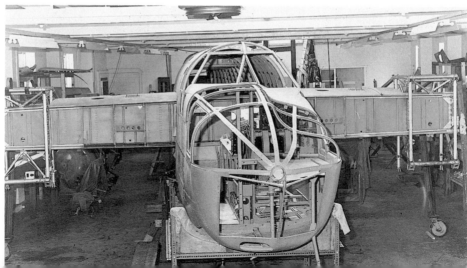

The whole centre-section was then completely re-skinned with new alloy panels, but on both centre and outer wing sections we went up a gauge on the thickness of the alloy for the skin and used a size larger on the rivets too. These measures, along with the spar-capping, led to a significant increase in the strength of the whole wing structure.

The new skin panels were cut using the old ones as patterns where possible. Each rivet hole was back-drilled into the new skin panels using the original holes in the ribs, stringers, etc, as a guide, before the re-riveting. Rivet pins were placed in alternate holes to hold the panel in position while the first stage of this operation was carried out. Then these pins were removed, the remaining holes back-drilled and the rest of the re-riveting on each new panel completed.

It doesn't take very long to describe this work but it took many, many months actually to carry out! The interior had all been etch-primed as we went along, and then painted green; and the exterior was etch-primed too and awaited painting.

The centre-section was then moved next door into the main workshops in 'Blenheim Palace'. To do this we fitted wheels to the four legs of the jig. We also had to move the brick piers that supported the lintel over the doors at the end of the Building 66 workshops outwards and enlarge the doors sufficiently to allow the centre section through, but even then it would only go through diagonally.

Work could then proceed to fabricate two new engine fire-resistant bulkheads. On the original aircraft these had been of an alloy and asbestos sandwich type of construction, but we elected to use a more modern stainless steel one, almost our only departure from original construction methods. This very tricky work, for stainless steel is very difficult to work by hand, was carried out by 'Smudger' Smith.

The circular, tubular engine-mounting frames forward of the front spar were subject to the same series of operations as the main tubular structures between the spars, and when completed they were inspected, tested and certified by BAe at Hatfield, and then bolted on to the new bulkheads: another major step forwards.

In the meantime both the fin and the one-piece tailplane with its twin spars, had been stripped right down and painstakingly restored in the same manner as all the other alloy structures and were ready to be reunited. Then the whole tail assembly was rebuilt on to the rear fuselage section, after all had been etch-primed and painted internally.

The rudder had been very badly damaged over the years, and was rebuilt using original Bristol drawings to fabricate the many new parts needed. It was

Above left *The port undercarriage mounting frame of square steel tubing, with oleo legs in the retracted position. The hydraulic actuating ram is in the centre of the picture, the rear of the front spar to the left, and the (empty) fuel tank bay to the right.*

Left *The rebuilt nose and rear fuselage re-united with the centre-section of 10038, showing the undercarriage mounting frames before the engine mountings were replaced and the new firewalls fabricated.*

An early stage of building up the moulds required for the glazing, utilizing the unused nose of 9893, the 'spare' airframe.

The scalloped nose fully glazed with the complex double-curved moulded perspex glazing and the flat toughened-glass bomb-aiming windows. The venturi tube for the stand-by vacuum source is on the side of the cockpit.

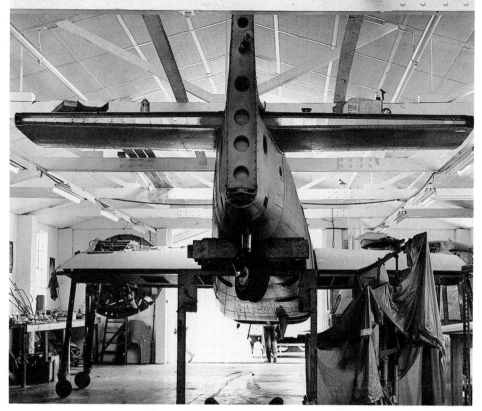

The stern section with the rebuilt fin, tailplane and tail-wheel mounted on the rear fuselage. Note the fin-post which runs from the base of the stern section of the fuselage up between the rafters. Compare this with the upper photograph on page 75.

then recovered with new fabric — we used Ceconite fabric not Irish linen, as it lasts far longer — and doped silver until it tightened to a drum-like tautness.

The castoring tail-wheel assembly itself had been stripped and rebuilt. The hydraulic shock-absorber strut had leather seals which still functioned, the castings, forks and mounting brackets had been X-rayed and crack-tested, new bearings both for the wheel and the swivelling strut were located and fitted, plus a new Blenheim tail-wheel tyre which had been donated by the Norwich Aviation Museum.

Another major item of restoration that had been proceeding meanwhile was the reconditioning of the main undercarriage assemblies. We had worked on a selection of 10 of the large oleo struts, they were then charged with hydraulic fluid to their very high working pressure and re-inspected and tested repeatedly until we were able to certify four of the main oleos as being serviceable. We had also inspected and crack-tested all the other parts of the complicated retractable undercarriage mechanism with its many links, bracing tubes and cables, hydraulic jacks, mounting brackets, etc.

All the components were polished before being repainted silver and the reconditioned and new-looking complete undercarriage units were then re-assembled with all new nuts and bolts and were ready to re-attach to their

The rear and stern fuselage complete with fin, tailplane and tailwheel is moved from the workshops into the hangar on a damp evening.

rebuilt mounting structures in the wheel bays behind the front spar.

Now that all the restored sections were together in a very crowded 'Blenheim Palace' we carried out a trial assembly, by mounting the nose and middle fuselage sections on to the wing centre section, complete with its engine mountings and bulkheads, then adding the rear fuselage section, with its tailwheel and the beautifully curved fin and rudder. We hit a snag here as the centre section was from 9893 and the fuselage sections were from 10038, and the keel-plate was obviously not jig-built originally but hand-fitted and would not fit. Considerable modification and redrilling was required to make it fit properly.

The undercarriage assemblies (less the main wheels) were bolted into place and retracted or extended manually whilst the retracting mechanism and the 'up' and 'down' locks were being adjusted. The characteristic Blenheim undercarriage fairing doors were rebuilt and re-attached. This was all very satisfying and worthwhile progress and it looked really magnificent. At last, too, it was now instantly recognizable as a Blenheim.

Another time-consuming but important task, carried out largely by Roy Pullan, the pilot on the Blenheim's last flight, was the construction of the moulds from which we could make the new double-curved glazing for the cockpit and nose. This again took years rather than months, but it was vital to get them absolutely right because not only did the resultant glazing have to be strong enough to withstand aerodynamic forces but it also had to give clear and undistorted vision — unlike the glazing on the Blenheim in the RAF museum, for example. This was achieved by filling the entire unrestored nose of the other Blenheim airframe 9073 with expanded polystyrene foam on suitable wooden bases and then carefully shaping and smoothing down the hardened foam in all three planes to the exact required profiles.

Female fibreglass moulds were then made directly from the accurately shaped mainly double-curved areas we had recreated, broken down into individual sections as required by the use of separate wooden bases, and all finished — indeed polished — to a fine and completely smooth surface. Male moulds in fibreglass on wooden formers were then made from these, again smoothed down to an unblemished finish, because any errors or marks in the moulds would be reproduced when the heated Perspex was shaped in them.

However, the resultant set of moulds were so accurate and well finished that we were able to produce from them complete sets of the complex double-curved Perspex glazing panels that were not only the correct shape but also were virtually optically perfect. We sold a set to another museum who were restoring a static Blenheim, which helped to defray some of the expense.

Incidentally, this is an area where we can save a lot of time on the second restoration, for we still have these moulds and it is relatively easy to produce a new set of glazing panels from them, compared with the long time it took to make the moulds in the first place.

The complete fuselage was now some 42 ft (13 m) long, and the centre section some 20 ft (6 m) wide, whilst the fin poked up between the roof trusses. Many was the visitor who said 'You'll never get it out through the doors!' But we did, for the main airframe sections were dismounted and moved into the hangar for re-assembly.

The wing centre section was placed on trestles first, then the nose, rear fuselage and stern frame sections — the latter complete with tailplane, fin and rudder — were carefully lined up. Then the joints were bolted together and the main sections were finally and permanently reunited with each other.

This represented a major step forward indeed.

Chapter Ten

Vital systems

Throughout the years of restoration, work had been moving forward on reconditioning and installing the various systems that were needed to transform the Blenheim from being a bare but empty airframe into a fully functioning, airworthy aircraft. Some of these vital systems have been mentioned in passing, but now need to be considered in greater detail.

The 12 volt electrical system had to be redesigned and renewed completely to take into account more recent developments, as well as for safety considerations. While we wanted to keep the aircraft as original as possible, we also needed to take advantage of modern avionics and the better, more reliable electrical equipment now available. This modified electrical system was devised by Colin Swann and executed by him, Hugh Smith and Christian Hollyer.

Electrical power is supplied by a 500 watt dc generator, driven by the port engine, to a 12 volt 25 amp general-services battery in the rear fuselage. There is also a 25 amp engine-starter battery under the navigator's seat. Remember that the Blenheim was built in the days when aircraft and cars had old-fashioned generators not alternators. The generator itself was sent away to a specialist for rewinding and overhaul, new 35 amp batteries were purchased and the circuits adapted to suit them.

All the old wiring had been stripped out and the whole aircraft was rewired with all new cables, connectors and relays, using the original alloy trunking to run it through. This is linked to the main fuse-box and electrical panel which is mounted in the rear fuselage forward of the wireless operator/air gunner's position, and was controlled by him. Mounted on this panel are the large master-switch for isolating the supply from the batteries, the fuses, the voltage-regulator, charging-rate controls and cut-outs, ammeters and voltmeter.

The original Blenheims had their old valve radios in the rear fuselage behind the turret. We deleted this and all the associated wiring, as well as the trailing aerial, and the signalling, bomb-arming circuits, and other redundant circuits.

The starter buttons are in the cockpit, as are the starter booster-coil buttons and a panel for the starter relays and fuses; the starters needed heavy-duty wiring, and we fitted 'starter-engaged' warning lights in the cockpit as a safety measure. Many of the engine instruments are electrically operated, as are the flap and undercarriage position indicators, plus the trim-tab position indicators for both elevators and rudder.

Electrical supplies, fuses, relays and controls are also needed, for navigation and formation lights (on nose, wingtips and rudder), cockpit and rear compartment internal lighting, instrument lighting, Pitot tube heating, the landing lamps and all the radio equipment, which gives some idea of the amount of rewiring and circuitry involved.

To facilitate operations in present-day controlled airspace, we fitted modern transistorized radio equipment, hidden in a panel down to the left of the pilot's seat (which was previously used for bomb arming and selection switches) so that we could keep the cockpit looking as original as possible. This modern radio comprised a 720 channel VHF set, a 720 channel nav/com set with VOR indicator, and a transponder. The special aerials required were also hidden as far as possible.

We designed and fitted a new intercom system from the cockpit to the two navigation positions (alongside the pilot and in the nose), to two rear positions (in the turret and at the fuselage electrical-station position used for take-off and

The complete centre-section mounted in the hangar with the rear fuselage and rudder. The civilian registration is applied. Note the oil tanks above the undercarriage mounting frames, and the row of D-shaped brackets on the front of the spar.

The main electrical panel inside the rear fuselage with charging-rate dials and controls; the pale intrusions beyond it are the canvas seals for the external footholds to the walkway on the wing. The Master Switch is top centre, and the curved trunking (here without its covering panels) leads the cabling to the main fusebox.

landing), and to each of the undercarriage bays (to be able to communicate with the engineers who, on starting, primed the engines externally from them). The latter was another safety related addition that we incorporated.

So it can be seen that the total amount of rewiring with all the modifications and improvements incorporated in the electrical circuits, resulted in a great amount of highly specialized and time-consuming work.

Air under pressure is used in one of the main systems, the wheel-brakes. It was also used originally for the fuel-jettison valves and the wing gun-firing and nose camera operating mechanisms, but we deleted those parts of the pressure circuit as redundant. A vacuum system is used for various flight instruments. It is vital of course that both systems are completely airtight and leak-proof for them to function correctly.

The vacuum system has a pump on the port engine, the circuit runs via an oil separator and suction relief valve, and powers the gyroscopic flight instruments. There is an alternate source from a venturi on the outside of the nose, pilot-controlled by a selector valve with its own relief valve, in case of engine or vacuum pump failure. The negative pressure in the system is shown on an indicator, tapped from downstream of the control valve, on the instrument panel.

The air pressure source is a compressor driven by the starboard engine, and its circuit runs (via an oil-trap and oil-reservoir) to a storage bottle in the centre section by the main-spar; an air-filter and ground-charging point are incorporated in this circuit near the storage bottle. The pressure in the system is regulated by a complicated valve and indicated on a triple-gauge in front of the pilot which shows the pressure in the system and the available individual brake pressures.

An emergency system is used to lower the undercarriage should the hydraulics (or the port engine) fail. It comprises a pressurized CO_2 bottle in each wheel bay, connected via a shuttle valve first to the 'unlock' side of the radius-rod lock-jack and then to the 'down' side of the main undercarriage jacks. It is operated (once only!) by pull controls behind the pilot's left shoulder. These three systems were overhauled most thoroughly, and tested carefully to ensure perfect operation.

The reason I said 'or the port engine' above is that there is only one hydraulic pump and that is driven by the port engine. There is a hydraulic reservoir, and a hand-pump for emergency use, and (in the event of a major hydraulic leak and loss of pressure) the pilot could use the emergency bottle to lower the wheels, but would be unable to use the flaps for his single-engined landing, or, in wartime, to use the turret to defend the aircraft.

The main and hand-pumps each have filters and relief valves and the hand-pump has a non-return valve. The hydraulic selector in the cockpit, to divert pressure (indicated by a dial on the instrument panel) to the undercarriage/flap circuit, to the powered turret, or back to the reservoir, has been described earlier. The hydraulic pressure system therefore was another which required the most careful reconditioning, rendered troublesome by the fact that the fluid attacks paint so any leaks were potentially damaging.

One of the other essential systems is the Pitot static system which provides vital information to the pilot by operating the altimeter and the air-speed and climb-and-descent indicators. This is done by comparing pressures supplied from the electrically heated Pitot/static head mounted on a mast beneath the nose via a circuit of air-tight light-alloy tubes to the instruments on the 'blind flying' panel. This mast also contains a resistance bulb to provide outside air-temperature indication.

The lines originally supplied slave air-speed and altitude instruments in both navigator's and gunner's positions, but we deleted these as an unnecessary complication in the rebuilding process.

The other essential is an engine fire-extinguisher system, which consists of a large CO_2 bottle in the fuselage with its outlet controlled by a selector valve on the instrument panel. It discharges the contents, via more 'plumbing', into the engine compartment and carburettor intake of whichever engine was selected by the valve before 'the knob was pulled' to operate the extinguisher system.

The remaining major system that had to be rebuilt throughout, and with the utmost care, was that for operating the flying controls. From the pilot's 'spectacle' type control-column the ailerons are controlled by a system of chains, sprockets and tie-rods connecting to levers mounted on the front of the main-spar. These levers operate torque tubes running outboard which connect to adjustable links and the aileron-operating levers, via a differential assembly.

The control column is pivoted at its base and moved backwards or forwards to operate the elevators via an adjustable control-tube to a transverse lever assembly under the central pedestal, from where a set of tensioned cables runs through a system of pulleys and guides to a similar lever assembly in the stern section of the fuselage which activates a vertical control-tube attached to the elevator operating lever. The whole of this cable-and-pulley run is duplicated for safety reasons, and we used new, carefully tensioned cables throughout.

The rudder is operated from pendant pedals, via the Dunlop brake-balance valve mentioned earlier, turning a vertically mounted torque-tube from which levers and rods operate a transverse lever assembly system (similar to the elevator controls) from which a duplicated set of cables run direct via pulleys to the rudder-operating arms. The trim tabs on both rudder and elevators are operated from cockpit hand-wheels via a system of chains, sprockets and cables to screw-jacks. All of these tail control runs pass from the central pedestal in the cockpit, through the roof of the bomb-bay, under the floor by the turret, and down the open centre of the rear fuselage.

There are two other main systems, both equally essential to flight of course, that had to be completely and scrupulously overhauled so that they too functioned perfectly — the fuel and oil systems! But as these systems supply the engines with the two fluids absolutely vital to their continued functioning, I will describe how they both were refabricated and reworked when covering the installation of the engines themselves following completion of the individual engine rebuilds.

Incidentally, when talking about the 'nuts and bolts' of working on the restoration, consideration must be given to those items themselves, for they

were a constant source of difficulty. When originally designed and manufactured the Blenheim naturally used imperial weights and measures, so the
dimensions were in feet, inches and fractions of an inch (down to thousandths
of an inch in some engine measurements) and it was built to the then current
British Standards (BS). So the AGS (Aircraft General Stores) classified sizes of
nuts, bolts, fittings, connections, rivets, etc, were used. These comprised the
BA (British Association) range, which had metric threads, BSF (British
Standard Fine) range and some of the Whitworth range — none of which was
compatible with another. The Canadians then complicated matters further by
using, in addition to all of these, some American UNF (United National Fine)
and UNC (United National Coarse) sizes, when they built the aircraft under
licence during the war.

So the team were faced with an incredible mixture of early British and
American sizes many of which were very difficult, if not impossible, to obtain.
Where practicable we tried to regularize the position by using the more readily
available American UNF, and British AN range of sizes. Rivet sizes are still
measured in fractions of an inch.

The majority of the electrical connections had BA sizes and threads, while
most of the many pipe fittings were BS, some were AN and a few UNC. We
now use AN where possible. The thickness of the alloy sheets used for the skins
and the steel used on the spar booms etc, was originally measured on the old
SWG (Standard Wire Gauge) scale but is now measured in thousandths of an
inch — although 22 gauge, for example, isn't anything as simple as 22
thousandths!

As for the many different tube sizes and materials, used in the flying-control
systems for example, with their multitude of varying diameters, lengths, wall-
thicknesses and end-fittings, this became a minefield that was only crossed with
the exercise of much patience and ingenuity.

Chapter Eleven

Preparing the engines

We must now go back in time to when the centre section was moved out from the adjacent workshops and into 'Blenheim Palace', for that was when we set about turning those workshops into a proper engine shop. 'Chalky' White was now working two or three days every week on the engines and he helped to lay out and organize the shop. Benches and sets of metal shelves were erected, vices, surface-plates, pressure-cleaning baths, compressed-air and electricity points installed. Engine hoists, and several stands were made, plus two special engine-building frames from old engine-mountings.

The mountain of old airframe parts were moved into storage, and all 19 of the derelict engines were moved into the shop; quite a bit of humping as the lads said. Of the 19 engines, some were relatively complete power plants still in their frames and with the exhaust collector-rings on the front, some were bare engines out of their frames with many parts missing, even some cylinders. All were very rusty and seized solid. We also had just the cores of four other engines, but these were virtually useless.

We had previously tried to remove some of the cylinders on the least derelict looking of the engines with but little success. When the cylinder barrels were unbolted they could not be removed as the cast iron piston-rings had rusted themselves on to the steel cylinder bores. Don't forget that these engines had stood out in all weathers through over 40 Canadian winters. Even if the odd cylinder was left on the compression or firing stroke with the valves closed, which kept the elements out, other cylinders would have open valves, letting in the damp air or worse. Many had had the platinum-tipped spark-plugs removed which let in the elements anyway! We discovered over a dozen mice skeletons and remains in various cylinders, where they had entered via an open valve and been unable to climb the smooth bore to get out again.

An engine being stripped in the dummy frame, with all the cylinders and ancillaries removed. Its number is chalked on the reduction-gear housing so that all the items removed can be tagged with the same number.

Three cylinder barrels with the remains of a dozen mice removed from them!

Above *Another engine in the hoist having the cylinders removed. Note the tagged barrels and pistons on the shelves.*

Top right *Shelves full of reclaimed cylinders and matching pistons, all numbered and resulting from many, many months of work. Note the two halves of an alloy supercharger casing on the lower shelf.*

Above right *A fine view of a part-rebuilt engine showing the crankshaft (with protective capping), the master con rod (behind the counter-weight), the eight articulated rods (taped for protection), and the rear-half of the split crankcase.*

Right *The front half of the crankcase (which fits on to the rear half shown in the previous picture) showing the pairs of push-rod mountings opposite each bore centre.*

Filling the cylinder above the piston with oil and/or de-rusting fluids and standing the engines with the cylinder being treated at the top, sometimes with the whole engine suspended on the one cylinder, freed quite a few.

Removing the rockers assemblies allowed the valve springs to close the valves, and by pumping the oil under considerable pressure in through a plug hole, we were able to free a few more. This was quite dangerous as sometimes they let go with quite a bang! Frequently several attempts or a combination of these methods used in sequence was necessary. Sometimes just one particularly stubborn cylinder on an engine would prove impossible to free, despite prolonged and great efforts, and an otherwise promising-looking engine would have to be disregarded. Often the steel cylinder barrels removed with such difficulty were corroded beyond hope of reclamation.

'Chalky' beavered away at this for many months, helped mainly by John Romain, until there were rows of reclaimable cylinder barrels, each numbered with its associated piston, on the shelves ready to be inspected and worked on. By then he also had several bare crankcases available for inspection, so that he could select the most suitable to form the basis for the engine rebuilds. The pistons themselves and their gudgeon-pins were all cleaned and examined in minute detail, including crack-testing of course, so that fully serviceable items could be selected.

The alloy crankcases are made in two halves joined at the bore centre lines, and are beautifully machined. After a most thorough cleaning and inspection, all were found to be well within the manufacturer's own tolerance figures, so did not present a problem, and 'Chalky' selected the very best ones to use. The front and rear covers, the supercharger, auxiliary-drive and reduction-gear casings too presented few problems, as nearly all of these alloy components were found to be completely in order, although some of the oil-collector sumps, which had magnesium casings, were in poor external condition.

Likewise, we had sufficient crankshafts available to select three with absolutely no measurable wear or run-out, after inspecting, X-raying and crack-testing them in great detail. They are a work of art, machined all over to the highest standards, indeed to a polished finish, as are the master and eight articulated rods, which were subjected to the same processes. The radii for the webs of these H-section forged steel connecting rods in particular are most beautifully machined. The many hours each one must have taken to manufacture originally and the high cost would not be tolerated in present-day production methods. Again, after the most searching examination we had sufficient connecting rods available to be able to select perfect sets.

The massive crankshaft roller main-bearings, and the big and small-end plain bearings in the articulating rods were found to be all well within their tolerances too. By then, with one major exception, we had all the basic components needed for the two main engines and the spare unit that we intended to build. The major problem that faced us with the engines was ascertaining if we did have sufficient serviceable cylinder barrels and pistons.

'Chalky' stripped the rocker-gear and valves from all the cylinders, again carefully numbering them. He made a jig to mount the cylinders on, and by

The rear of the engine, showing the supercharger casing, feeding the mixture from the carb (which fits on to the manifold at the lower centre) into the eye of the supercharger impeller.

fitting a wooden T-handle as a gudgeon pin in a spare piston, he made a tool used with fine paste and polish to hone the bores. He spent many, many months patiently lapping pistons, including the two master-pistons, into the cylinders until they were a perfect fit. All were weighed and balanced to fractions of an ounce.

After these lengthy and painstaking efforts we were fortunate to end up with all the 18 cylinders required for the first two engines, complete with their perfectly matching pistons, externally powder-blasted and painted, all tagged and sitting on the shelves in virtually new condition.

Above left *A partially rebuilt engine, awaiting the cylinders, reduction-gear and casing, manifolds, etc. The picture on page 96 shows the same engine complete, and that on page 109 shows it installed on the airframe.*

Left *The front of the crankcase with one reclaimed cylinder mounted on it, showing the annular camshafts and rollers that actuate the push-rods.*

Above *'Chalky' White with John Romain fitting a reconditioned cylinder. The 'Old Master' passed on a wealth of expertise to his apt young pupil.*

The only new parts used on the entire engines, apart from nuts and bolts, were the piston rings themselves, which we had specially manufactured by Wellworthy using salvaged examples as patterns. It speaks volumes for the very high standard of construction of those old wartime engines, left lying about uninhibited for all those years in extreme weather conditions, that we were able to use all the other engine components.

Then came the long task of carefully grinding in 36 valves in each engine, again performed with patience and a refusal to accept anything that wasn't absolutely spot on. As mentioned, he would leave each cylinder inverted with the valves closed and use the leaking petrol test to ensure that the seals were perfect on all four valve-seats. The triple valve springs for each valve were checked and measured before re-assembly.

Similarly, 'Chalky' thoroughly examined the inlet and exhaust cams on their gear-driven drum, carefully measuring the lift of each lobe; plus the rocker arm,

The engine shown on page 94, virtually complete. Note the taped-off exhausts that lead to the collector-ring. The oil-pipe above the reduction-gear casing is for the prop pitch change. The alloy sump (bottom centre) feeds the oil scavenge pumps which return the oil to the dry-sump oil-tank.

roller-tappet and push-rod assemblies. The machined rocker arms operate in roller bearings, another example of what today would be considered over-engineering.

We were indeed glad that the engines were so beautifully made with such an apparent disregard for the high cost of the large amount of skilled labour and top-grade materials required, for they would not have lasted nearly so well if they had been built to the more cost-conscious 'efficiency' of present-day production methods.

The pair of magnetos for each engine and the single generator had been sent away to a specialist for rewinding and complete overhaul, and they came back as good as new. The gear-and-shaft spring drives for all of them were checked and overhauled, with their respective bearings. This was also done with the

Above *Port wing mounted in the jig, de-skinned but not all paint-stripped. Repairs have started at the root end, and five of the trailing-edge ribs, above the empty tank bay, have been renewed.*

Below left *Close-up of a just-removed cylinder and piston, showing the mess in the bore and over the valves in the head, plus a dead mouse and rubbish that was above the piston, and the gummed-up piston rings.*

Below right *Edgar White and John Smith in the engine shop. 'Chalky' has his hand on a part-rebuilt engine.*

Above *Royal visit — The Queen Mother was most interested in the Blenheim. Here Ted Inman, Keeper of the Imperial War Museum at Duxford, presents first John Romain, then the rest of the Blenheim team.*

Below *First roll-out for the press in July 1986. The Blenheim, in yellow etch-primer, is still less the outer wings, bomb-doors and nacelles.*

Right *As the day of the first engine-runs approached, the team worked harder than ever. John and Billy are working on the port engine and Robert is inserting the cooling-gill plates. The rig for priming with warmed oil is on the lower right.*

Left *As completion neared, work in the hangar often continued late into the night. Note the glow from the heat-lamps under the engines.*

Below left *The great day when both engines were run together for the first time.*

Above *Interior of the Blenheim cockpit viewed from the pilot's entrance hatch. Note the ring-and-bead gunsight, the P11 Compass (compare with picture on page 67) and the engine controls on the centre console.*

Below *John Larcombe and John Romain taxy out for their pre-take-off checks before another successful test flight.*

Bottom *'Larks' brings the Blenheim over the Duxford runway threshold prior to rounding out for a beautiful landing. The large trailing-edge flaps are in the fully down position.*

Above *John Romain gives scale to the port Bristol Mercury engine; both are cooling down after a test flight that included single-engine climbs.*

Above right *Chief pilot John Larcombe, a British Airways Training Captain, ponders over the charging problem with Billy and John, after a test flight.*

Right *Fine air-to-air shot of the Blenheim taken from the Beech 18. The two Johns are in the cockpit and Bill in the turret. Note that the engine cooling gills are closed for cruising flight.*

'We laid out the wreckage in the hangar.'

'The rear fuselage was broken off at the turret.'

'The nose had vanished.'

The smashed cockpit from which John Romain was ejected.

Right The packed area between the rear of the engine and the 'firewall'; oil-cooler and outlet at the top, inlet manifolds left, generator (tagged) to the right of the magneto, and hand-crank drive lower centre.

Left *A completed engine being taken to the hangar by Hugh Smith and Christian Hollyer, with 'Terence the Tug'.*

Below left *The starboard engine installed, showing the inner cowling which guides the airflow to the controllable cooling gills. The nose perspex is taped over for protection.*

Bottom left *A clear view of the cooling-gills in relation to the inner cowling, and of the exhaust 'collector-ring' system and one of its two outlets. The two circular intakes are ducted to the oil-cooler.*

Below *Happiness is Big Bristols! Smudge's photo of the completed Bristol Mercury as used on the Blenheim T-shirts.*

drives for the air compressors, the vacuum and hydraulic pumps, and the main fuel and oil pump — which provides both pressure and scavenge — for each engine. Each one of these vital units was individually stripped, cleaned, examined, checked, measured, rebuilt, calibrated and tested, until finally cleared as fit for use.

The centrifugal supercharger is another minor work of art. The circular impellor is driven via triple epicyclic spring-clutches, from the rear of the crankshaft. It accepts mixture from the carburettor centrally and centrifugal force expels it under pressure tangentially into beautifully curved volutes or channels (formed and machined in both halves of the two-part alloy supercharger casing) that lead into similarly curved inlet manifolds.

The impeller is most accurately machined and very finely balanced, and its shaft runs in roller bearings. It is geared up to several times engine speed; in fact at the cruising rpm of 2,400 the impeller is spinning round at over 22,500 rpm! In view of this, the supercharger assemblies were all examined and measured most meticulously, and then re-assembled with the greatest care. We had read that because of the wide temperature range and this high rotational speed these impeller bearings can wear excessively, especially on starting the engines from cold. To overcome this we arranged an extra oil-feed to each bearing, so that we could prime them with pre-warmed oil before starting.

'Chalky' started building up one engine on a stand in his bay, and John Romain followed on building up the other in the bay alongside. At each step, he first of all showed John exactly what he was doing and explained it fully, before he supervised John carrying out the same operation. By this means he was able to pass on much of his rare and invaluable experiences and much of his almost unrivalled expertise to the much younger engineer. The standard of his workmanship was exemplary and his knowledge of aircraft piston-engines profound, so it is to his great credit that he was willing to demonstrate the one and to share the other so readily.

In this the team was far more fortunate than we realized at the time, for as mentioned when the members of the team were being introduced to readers, we lost poor 'Chalky' soon after the engine rebuilds were completed and sadly he did not live long enough to hear them run. He would have been proud of them, for they both ran beautifully.

However, well before the first engine was completed, a dramatic development was to throw the whole Blenheim restoration into doubt and confusion.

Chapter Twelve

A dramatic development

The costs of the restoration had been mounting steadily over the years, for at that stage we had received virtually no help from the aviation industry. The Blenheim project stood in my garage company's books at well over £200,000 but would, when completed, be an asset worth more so it was a viable undertaking, although I had no intention of ever realizing its value by putting it on the market.

However, we were in for a sudden shock and a traumatic experience that resulted in the team very nearly losing the partially restored Blenheim altogether, and for many months it looked most unlikely that it would ever be completed to fly again.

The private company that had financed the rebuilding was itself the subject of an enforced take-over on 15 November 1984. The new owners were not interested in taking over the restoration project and wanted the book value for it. The other aircraft operated by the British Aerial Museum were personally owned by myself and not by the company so were not affected, but the future of the Blenheim project hung very much in the balance. This was all most disturbing and upsetting for me and, quite understandably, completely demoralized the team.

The accountants involved put the uncompleted Blenheim restoration project out to public tender, seeking to realize a price far higher than the best I had been able to offer. We assisted them to prepare a report on what work had been done and what remained to do. The closing date for tenders was twice extended due, they said, 'to strong interest from overseas' — so the period of worrying uncertainty was drawn out further.

The thought of the Blenheim, which we regarded very much as 'our Blenheim' as all of us in our own way had put so much into it, leaving Duxford for some unknown foreign destination was quite unbearable. The team rallied

Top *The completed and glazed nose section masked for priming.*

Above *The primed nose in the hangar being offered up to centre-section . . .*

Below *. . . lined-up carefully . . .*

. . . and finally mated to the main fuselage and and centre section. This head-on view shows clearly the scalloped nose designed to improve the view of the pilot on take-off and landing.

round magnificently but we were unable to avoid or change this most unsatisfactory situation and felt frustrated and powerless.

The revised closing date for the formal submission of tenders drew near — 16 April 1985, a full five months after I had lost control of the company. I had put in a personal tender at the highest sum that I could reasonably afford, but I was very worried that it would not be high enough to succeed. So, after several more sleepless nights, I submitted a further tender in my name (wearing my British Aerial Museum hat) at a higher figure, which was just — but I understand only just — high enough to be successful.

Many months of nail-biting doubt and uncertainty, with the very real prospect of the team and me losing the Blenheim forever, were over at last. Had the partially completed restoration project been sold to another party we were not to know if they had the determination, the facilities, the expertise or the funding to complete it. It is quite possible that, faced with the manifold difficulties involved, the Blenheim would not have been completed to fly once more, and all our work and effort up to that time would have been wasted.

The joy of the team on hearing that the crisis was over, and that I had managed to rescue the Blenheim restoration from an unknown fate so that the rebuild would continue to completion in their very capable hands, was unbounded and made my own great efforts to secure that result worth while.

However, it did mean that I would have to finance the completion — and there was still a lot of work to be done — from my own pocket directly, rather than indirectly as before. Incidentally, the company had previously sold the components of the second Blenheim airframe to the Imperial War Museum at cost, for eventual rebuild as a static exhibit, with the proviso that the restoration team would have first choice of any parts that may be needed for the airworthy aircraft.

The company had also sold the team's first Chipmunk, which was so beautifully restored that it made a world record price at the Christie's auction at Duxford in 1983. However, this meant that the proceeds of neither sale were available to help fund the restoration of G-MKIV to airworthy status.

We began to seek more assistance and sponsorship from our suppliers, and to look at ways of doing as much as possible 'in house' rather than placing items with outside contractors. We began to scrounge, or buy as cheaply as possible, more of the materials needed; and to look for some outside work that would help to pay the overheads, including part of the wages of the full-time engineers. We pursued far more actively obtaining airshow and film or photographic work for our other aircraft.

An example of this approach was the job of repairing and pressure testing the main alloy fuel tanks. We had been quoted over £10,000 for this work so decided to do it ourselves! We had completed previously a similar task on the oil-tanks quite successfully. So both the fuel tanks were thoroughly purged, then re-welded and repaired as necessary, and new seals for the filler-caps were fabricated. Then the completed tanks were pressure tested and found to be fuel-tight — they even survived the major accident at Denham without rupturing. This was a tribute to the skill of the team.

Another major problem that we still had to overcome was the question of serviceable main-wheel tyres. Although the original tyres still had their wartime air in them and appeared to be in very good condition, we dare not risk using

Top right *The nose mated to the fuselage and centre-section, with protective clear plastic taped over the new glazing. Smudge, John and Christian Hollyer, with John Gullick and Colin Swann seated at the front.*

Above right *The rebuilt starboard engine with new inner cowlings is fitted, together with the rudder and elevators. Now it really looks like a Blenheim!*

Right *The main wheels are now also fitted; the undercarriage is in the semi-retracted position due to the height of the supporting trestles.*

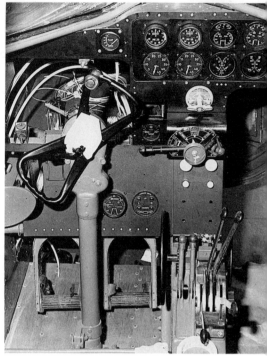

them in case one should burst on take-off or landing. Replacement tyres of the correct dimensions and rating were unobtainable anywhere, and Dunlops had long ago destroyed the moulds. Many alternatives were studied but none, for various reasons, was suitable.

Then Shorts of Belfast announced their new 360 Feederliner and to our delight the tyres were just what we needed! They were identical, apart from a ½ in increase in diameter, which was acceptable. So we purchased a new pair plus inner tubes and that particular problem, which may well have prevented the aircraft from becoming airworthy, was solved most fortuitously.

Prior to this we had overhauled the main-wheel axles and bearings, and selected serviceable examples of the alloy wheels themselves. The drum brakes were also reconditioned, skimming the rusted drums, renewing the air-lines, and finding sufficient unworn and oil-free brake-shoes.

The brakes are pneumatically operated by compressed air being fed into small inflatable rubber bags so that they expand behind multiple brake-shoes, forcing them against the drums. Crude but effective. Amazingly we found enough of these rubber bags to be airtight and in good condition to re-assemble both brake sets and have a few as spares, for if the brakes are overheated they easily burst.

The brakes were applied by a small lever behind the control column 'spectacles' being squeezed gently by thumb and fingers — difficult if the aircraft was bounding over an uneven grass airfield — with the amount of brake differential to either wheel being controlled by the position of the rudder

Far left *The interior of the rear fuselage, now painted, showing some of the control cables that run beneath the floor. The tailplane front-spar is at the rear top above the elevator-actuating arms and tail-wheel oleo.*

Left *The cockpit in the workshop. The 'blind-flying' instrument panel is not fitted, the circular mounting to the left is for the compass (see the picture on page 67), the engine instruments are upper centre, the engine controls lower centre, and the hydraulic-selector in the centre.*

Right *Looking aft from the nose, showing (centre) the hydraulic leads to the selector and the engine controls, with the rudder pedals beneath the nav table. The front spar runs across the background.*

Below *The starboard engine mounted with the centre-section leading edge and lower escape hatch (temporarily) fitted. The undercarriage is in the retracted position.*

pedals, as is common to all aircraft. On the Blenheim this is achieved by a complicated Dunlop pneumatic distribution valve linked to the rudder pedals, so that full left rudder meant all the braking going to the left wheel and vice versa. The first ever Blenheim accepted for squadron service was tipped on to its back and written off upon delivery when the unfortunate 114 Squadron pilot applied the brakes after landing at Wyton on 10 March 1937!

We were most fortunate indeed in that we persuaded British Aerospace at Lostock, formerly a factory for de Havilland Propellers, to rebuild the Blenheim propellers as a training exercise, for the commercial cost of such work would have been prohibitive. The props had in fact originally been built there in 1940; a check of the numbers stamped on them revealed that a very young man who worked on them then had subsequently risen to become Director of Production. They had travelled in a wartime convoy to Canada, then back to the UK some 30 years later, and completed the circle by returning to Lostock after 45 years!

The team had well and truly got the bit between their teeth now, and work continued in both the hangar and 'Blenheim Palace' at an ever-increasing pace as completion of the restoration came ever more clearly into sight.

The refurbished oil and fuel-tanks were installed and connecting up all the 'plumbing' with oil, fuel and hydraulic lines progressed.

The opening cooling-gill rings, which control the amount of cooling air passing through the cowlings and thus the engine operating temperatures, had been painstakingly rebuilt, largely by Christian Hollyer. The gills are a series of interleaved alloy plates mounted on to an annular steel frame by rotating forks which are driven by an endless chain (within the frame) so that the gills open and close. These drives were manually operated on early Blenheims by hand-cranks, sprockets and chains, but electrically operated on Canadian-built aircraft such as G-MKIV.

The control surfaces too had been completely rebuilt by then; the rudder was repaired, many new ribs made, new bearings for the pivots installed, the leading edge was re-skinned in alloy and the rest re-covered (with longer-lasting Ceconite fabric rather than the Irish linen of the original) and doped; the same thorough treatment was given to the elevators and both ailerons. All had to be carefully balanced. The rudder and elevators were then attached to the fin and tailplane, and the graceful curves of the Blenheim tail assembly admired by all.

The rebuilt main-undercarriage assemblies, with all their hydraulic rams, pipework and retracting mechanism and links, and now complete with wheels

Top right *Taken on the same day as the previous picture, but with the undercarriage legs extended, this photograph also shows the beautifully curved moulded perspex glazing panels.*

Above right *The port engine was fitted later. The 'spare' nose, used for making the glazing moulds, can just be seen under the gantry in the background. Note the control runs starting to be fixed on the 'D' brackets on the front of the main spar.*

Right *Now the exhaust-collector and cooling-gill rings have been added. The two circular intakes on the starboard side of each engine are for the oil-coolers. The rebuilt dorsal turret is fitted in the retracted position.*

A most unusual shot showing the main wheel in the retracted position. Note the inner cowling behind the cooling-gills and the oil tank at the top. The upper and lower nacelles complete the streamlined shape with only the cylinders projecting into the air-flow.

and brakes, were refitted to the undercarriage bays. The retractions and extensions were operated and adjusted, the 'up' and 'down' locks carefully set, and the correct functioning was tested with an external hydraulic jig supplying the pressure. It whirred away and the undercarriage retracted and extended with a loud, satisfying 'clunk' as the locks engaged.

It was quite fascinating to see and hear the Blenheim airframe becoming 'live' at last.

Chapter Thirteen

Wings and prayers

The most difficult part of the entire restoration was rebuilding the outer wings, for they had suffered very badly in their years of exposure to the elements. To make the airframes easier to move on the Canadian farms where most ended up, and because they were of little use anyway, the outer wings had been removed and left lying about on the ground; even if stacked on their leading edges water would enter and collect on the rear faces of the spars.

The laminated steel, angle-section booms at the top and bottom of the alloy spar webs and the steel cornices which provide further stiffening for them were particularly vulnerable to corrosion, even though painted originally. This had been a problem in the wing centre section, as described earlier, but not nearly as serious a problem as in the outer wings. The middle of the centre sections were protected by the fuselage, the outer parts behind the engines usually had a film of engine oil which helped preserve them better, and all were raised above the ground.

The curved cornices were a particular problem, for as the number of laminations in the booms lessened towards the wing-tips, so the cornices reduced in thickness and size until they ended completely about two-thirds along the outer wings. Unfortunately the ends were left open forming a tunnel right down to the wing roots, into which inquisitive rodents and insects made their way and their homes. Their urine was particularly corrosive over the years, and we found the worst areas were where their nests had been.

Once the fuselage and centre section were moved into the hangar we had room in 'Blenheim Palace' to tackle this major problem; only partial stripping of the two pairs of outer wings available had taken place up to that stage — and we did not like what we could see!

The starboard wing was the worst-looking of the pair we decided to use, and it was tackled first. A steel jig was constructed and bolted to the workshop

Above *The port wing showing the damage caused by Customs Officers axing through the skin and ribs the full length of each spar.*

Right *Paint-stripping — a long and messy job, and all done by hand. Here Colin is stripping and cleaning a wing-root rib.*

Far right *The underside of the wing, mounted in the jig, showing the severe damage to the trailing-edge ribs and the flap mountings.*

floor, which held the wing upright with the trailing-edge uppermost, and prevented any movement of the spars when the stressed-skin was removed.

This wing had been badly damaged by HM Customs Officers at Harwich axing through it in a fruitless 'search' — this vandalism was quite unnecessary as there are ample inspection panels available.

Once all the skin panels had been removed by drilling out each rivet individually, and the panels numbered for use as patterns when the replacement skin panels were fabricated, the whole structure was laboriously paint-stripped and cleaned so that a detailed inspection could take place. All the necessary repairs to the ribs with their flanged edges and lipped lightening holes, and to the top-hat section stringers, were carried out, most of the trailing-edge ribs had to be renewed as they were beyond salvage.

Damaged sections of the spar steel angle-booms and cornices were cut out and replaced with new sections of the specially treated and formed steel that Filton had supplied, using their Repair Manual schemes as with the centre section spars. The spars were protected, re-assembled and then capped with new shaped and treated steel strips, in the same manner as the centre section.

This capping is not quite as simple as it sounds. To ensure that the location is absolutely spot on, the old skin panels are temporarily refixed into position with rivet pins on the ribs and stringers, with the new spar capping clamped in place, and then the capping is back-drilled either from underneath via the rivet holes in the original spar flanges, or from above via the original rivet holes in the old skins. The old skins are then removed and the caps bonded, held by rivet pins, and finally riveted into the exact position required, after each hole has been enlarged by re-drilling to suit the one size larger rivets that we employed throughout the wings.

All was then primed and painted internally so that the new skin panels could be fabricated and fitted. These were made up of 22 SWG L72 alloy, thicker than the original 24 gauge material used. These skins too were located correctly by the laborious back-drilling process described above. The new and thicker skins, together with the extra spar-capping, resulted in wings that were considerably stronger than the originals.

The wing was removed from the jig, the curved tips with their wooden formers renewed, the rebuilt outer-flaps fitted, and the overhauled aileron controls fitted; the completed wing was then wheeled into the hangar.

We had previously looked at the port outer wing which was apparently in far better condition than the starboard outer wing. Some skins had been removed

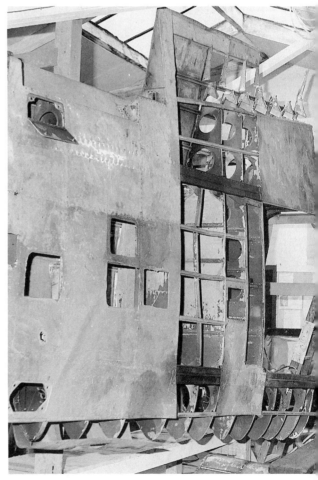

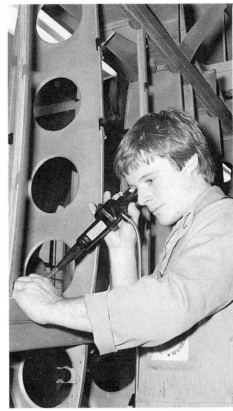

and external inspection of the spar-booms and cornices showed that they appeared to be in good condition. Several ribs, etc, had been repaired and a few new skin panels fitted, so we thought it would not take long to complete this wing too. However, we were in for a shock.

When it was mounted in the jig and the remainder stripped down, we decided to remove a couple of the cornices for a closer inspection. This was because we had made an internal inspection using a remote fibre-optic boroscope kindly loaned by KeyMed of Southend (an implement normally used for peering into people's stomachs!) and this had revealed areas of concern. This instrument was not available when we first looked at the port wing, though we had used it on the centre section and the starboard wing. Removing the two cornices revealed several areas of unexpected internal corrosion, so we removed the other six too, and found a few more. Some could be treated but others required replacement.

We had used the last of the lengths of the original special steel from Filton on the starboard wing, and they did not have nor could they obtain any more. We searched all the steel stockists for examples of it, or a modern equivalent, but without success, as that type of steel is just not used anymore.

We were put on to Krupps the giant German steelmakers near Essen, and the target of many RAF bombing raids during the war. We gave them the reference numbers of the specification, which they looked up in their records and said, 'Ah yes, zis steel was used on ze Blenheim, ze Beaufort and ze Beaufighter and confirmed that they could manufacture some for us. The only snag was that their minimum order was for 30 tons and we required only a few short lengths!

The chairman of British Steel on hearing of this arranged for one of their mills to produce a small batch and we were saved. We had to have these fabricated in a maximum of 6 ft lengths as these were the largest that we could have formed to shape and heat-treated. The material was supplied annealed to permit forming to the required complex angle and cornice profiles. This was done by Varne Engineering of Biggleswade who did an excellent job, using samples to obtain the desired profiles which varied throughout the length of the spars.

The shaped pieces were then re-treated by Mormet Heat Treatment Ltd of Brierly Hill in the West Midlands, by hardening and oil-quenching at 860°C and air-quenching at 460°. Test samples were cleared as meeting the original specification by British Aerospace at Filton. The CAA was kept informed throughout and approved this method of repairing the spars. It was all quite a performance but shows that a solution to most problems can be found.

Top far left *The tip-end of the wing in the steel jig. Note the shaped alloy blocks where it is bolted to the jig at the outer ends of the spars.*

Top left *John Romain using a fibre-optic scope to inspect the interior of the spar cornice.*

Left *The starboard wing in the jig, completely stripped and with the ribs rebuilt. The front spar (at the bottom of the picture) has been repaired and re-capped. The rear spar flanges and cornices have been removed for similar repair work.*

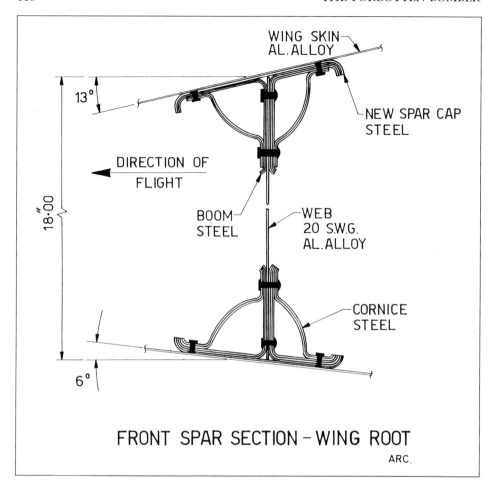

WING SKIN
AL. ALLOY

NEW SPAR CAP
STEEL

13°

DIRECTION OF
FLIGHT

18·00"

BOOM
STEEL

WEB
20 S.W.G.
AL. ALLOY

CORNICE
STEEL

6°

FRONT SPAR SECTION – WING ROOT

ARC.

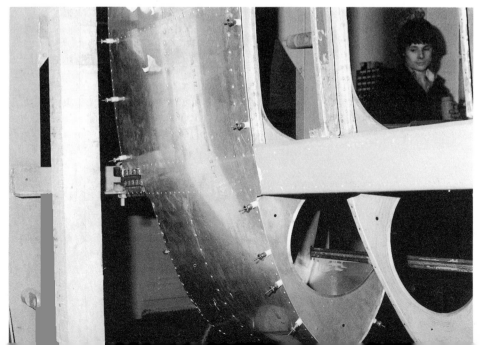

Following these spar repairs, the rest of port wing was then rebuilt and re-skinned in the same manner as the starboard wing and, somewhat belatedly, the completed wing was wheeled into the hangar for attachment to the airframe. All this extra and unexpectedly difficult work had delayed the team by many months.

The attachment lugs, forked eye-fittings, and main bolts for both sides were inspected radiographically by Quest Inspection of Luton Airport and cleared. They had also inspected and certified the engine frames and other parts. Then the lugs and fittings, plus the heavy-gauge triple-link plates and web-joint plates, were all bolted on with new nuts and bolts. These multi-bolted linking plates set the dihedral angle of the wing which is all on the outer planes.

The rebuilt port wing was finally fixed to the centre section many months after the starboard wing. The basic airframe was now complete.

Meanwhile throughout the lengthy period (some two years) that the wings took to rebuild in the workshops, work in the hangar on the fuselage and centre sections had proceeded apace.

First the rebuilt starboard and then the port power plants, mounted ready on their frames, had been proudly wheeled up to the hangar from the engine shop in turn, and attached to their respective engine mountings. They looked magnificent and were much admired. The completely reconditioned turret had been lowered into the fuselage by crane, and connected up; the four rebuilt hatches (two upper and two lower) were fitted, as were the graceful wing-root fairings.

Work continued on reconditioning, installing and 'plumbing in' the various systems described earlier. Hydraulic, pneumatic, electrical, flying and engine controls, vacuum, static, fuel and oil systems, cockpit fittings and instrument panels, all moved forward steadily. The exhaust manifolds, collector rings and outlet pipes were fitted, but we deleted the Canadian cabin-warming system. The cooling-gill rings and their operating controls were fitted.

The under-wing nacelles that fair in the retracted undercarriage were made up with mainly new, shaped panels. For the over-wing nacelles behind the engines, colloquially referred to as 'beetlebacks', we had to make up a wooden former and fabricate new ones to the Blenheim profile, as Canadian examples enlarged them to accommodate greater capacity oil-tanks and a dinghy-pack.

The rebuilt main fuel-tanks were installed, and the fuel feeds and three-way tank selectors on either side of the cockpit were connected up and plumbed in with all new fuel-lines, non-return valves, filters, connectors and fittings, as was the cross-feed system and its selector valves and fuel-lines.

The oil-tanks too had been stripped, cleaned and refurbished; they were

Top left *A drawing of the cross-section of a wing spar, showing the vertical alloy web (full height not depicted) with the difficult-to-form angles of the steel boom stiffeners and cornices; the additional spar 'capping' is also shown.*

Left *A new skin panel being fixed to repaired ribs at the root end of the wing; the reinforcing capping to the top of the front spar can be seen.*

Left *The completely rebuilt and functional Bristol B Mk 4 hydraulically-operated retractable dorsal turret with twin Browning .303 machine guns.*

Above *The interior of the rebuilt turret showing the breech-blocks of the twin Browning .303 guns. The ammo boxes are to either side, and the black rams raise and lower the entire turret independent of the movement of the gun mountings.*

connected with new oil-lines and fittings to the cylindrical oil-coolers. These had been most thoroughly flushed-out under pressure in a cleaning tank (and I mean for many weeks in different positions!), and fitted with a bypass for cold-starting, and connected via a pressure-relief valve and the Tecalamit oil-cleaners to the engines. The fuel gauges are activated by float-operated electrical transmitters and had to be carefully rebuilt and recalibrated.

We were delighted to collect the beautifully rebuilt propellers from British Aerospace at Lostock — their highly skilled craftsman had done an absolutely magnificent job — and mount them via a hoist on to the reduction-gear output shafts. At the end of a hard day's work the team just stood back and admired the Blenheim with its 'new' props gleaming.

At long last it really looked like the purposeful, yet aesthetically pleasing, high-performance war-plane that it had been all those years before.

Chapter Fourteen

Patience rewarded

In relating how the outer wings were mounted on the airframe, and the engines and propellers installed, I have not kept to the chronological sequence of events. It was easier when describing the work involved in rebuilding the wings to continue the narrative until they were completed and attached to the airframe, but in fact a lot of other work had been proceeding simultaneously before we had reached that stage.

Building up the engines was not just a case of mounting the reconditioned cylinders on the crankcase; the rest of the engines with all their drives and ancillaries had to be reconditioned too. The reduction gears, whose output shaft is splined into the propeller hubs, had to be stripped, examined, measured, checked most accurately for truth and lack of run-out, before reassembly into their alloy casings. The inlet tracts and manifolds, with their expansion joints, had to be refurbished and installed, as had the baffles between the cylinders, the ducts to the oil-coolers, and the exhaust manifolds and collector-rings.

The overhauled magnetos had to be assembled on their drives and timed carefully; and all-new shielded ignition harnesses were made and fitted. The reconditioned oil pumps, fuel pumps, compressors, vacuum pumps, hydraulic pumps, and generators, were all mated to their drives, re-fitted, tested and cleared.

The mounting-cones of pierced ¼ in alloy, which carry the weight of the engines and bolt to the circular engine-mounting frames; were checked, measured and re-mounted on the rear of the crankcases, where they are on the engine's centre of gravity.

Ten of the very complex Claudel-Hobson multi-jet carburettors, with their variable datum automatic boost and mixture control systems, were stripped right down, and sufficient components were reconditioned to assemble into

Right *The reduction-gears for the propeller, driven from the nose of the crankshaft, prior to strip, measurement, overhaul and rebuild.*

Below *One of the twin-choke carburettors laid out on the bench for inspection and measurement. Each one took months of meticulous work to overhaul and test thoroughly.*

three serviceable units. 'Chalky' constructed a fuel-flow rig so they could be checked, tested and calibrated against the manufacturer's figures in the manual. This task of reconditioning three carburettors (one for a spare) took many, many months of dedicated and highly skilled work. We knew that a restored Westland Lysander which uses the same Bristol Mercury engine had suffered from a lot of serious carburettor problems and we were determined to overcome them.

These carburettors have two very powerful accelerator pumps for each choke — these pumps squirt over three pints of neat fuel directly into the chokes as the throttles are being opened, to cater for the increased fuel demand of an accelerating engine, and a second pump has its similar action delayed by 1½ seconds to continue this temporary enrichment and help the engine to pick up cleanly. It follows that the throttles have to be opened progressively and carefully to avoid a 'rich cut' and allow this process to take place. On modern aircraft such as the 747, the pilot can slam the throttles wide open as quickly as he wishes and a device automatically controls the rate of opening to the optimum amount — not so on a Blenheim. The problems of getting a 25-litre engine to accelerate cleanly in those days were immense, for the Mercury was first tested in 1921 and engine technology (such as fuel-injection replacing carburettors) has advanced enormously since then.

We had to fabricate complete new carburettor intakes, with their alternate hot-air selection flaps and vanes, as the Canadian intakes were different to those used on Blenheims. They were made and welded up from mild-steel sheet by 'Smudger'. The circuit which supplies engine oil to heat the areas around the chokes that were particularly liable to carburettor icing was most carefully cleaned, inspected and tested.

We had been honoured by a visit from HM Queen Elizabeth the Queen Mother (see page 44), and the team were delighted to be presented. Her Majesty was impressed with the work, remembered Blenheims well from the war, and recalled attending the first investiture of the war with HM King George VI to award DFCs to Blenheim crews. Later we enjoyed a visit by HRH Prince Andrew and Miss Sarah Ferguson, just before she became Duchess of York, who were most interested in the Blenheim and asked a lot of pertinent questions.

When the engines were installed on the airframe, all the engine controls had to be made and connected up both in the cockpit and on the engines. These were the throttle, boost, carb heat, mixture and propeller-pitch controls, carb cut-outs, fuel cocks and cross-feed selectors, ignition switches, cooling-gill and oil-cooler shutter controls, starters and starter boost-coils. Plus of course the complete oil and fuel-systems mentioned earlier; not to forget all the connections from the engines to the hydraulic, pneumatic, vacuum, cooling-gill and fire-extinguisher systems.

We were very fortunate in that Teleflex Ltd installed their flexible controls for throttles and mixtures, to the original Blenheim specification, from the end of the airframe system of rods and levers to the actual controls on the engines, in place of the Canadian Arens push/pull controls, as the Teleflex controls operate much more smoothly and accurately. They also fitted Aerolux crew harnesses with Teleflex inertia reels which were much better and more comfortable to wear than the original Sutton harness. Little did we know that they would be violently tested so soon.

The engine instruments themselves had all been reconditioned and now had to be connected up at both ends. They were rpm indicators, boost gauges, oil pressure and temperature, fuel pressure, cylinder-head and carb intake temperatures; pneumatic and brake pressures, vacuum and hydraulic pressures.

The flight instruments too were overhauled, re-calibrated and certified before installing in the sprung-mounted 'blind flying panel' and then connecting up: the airspeed indicator, altimeter and rate of climb indicator to the pitot/static system; the artificial horizon, directional giro, and turn-and-bank indicators to the vacuum system. The electrical instruments as well were tested and installed; the flap, undercarriage and trim-position indicators; fuel gauges and several of the engine instruments.

All the other ancillary controls and switches in the cockpit were also connected or wired up. We were lucky to find an original P11 compass which was mounted in the correct position; we also fitted a standby compass and a VOR indicator. We installed an accellerometer to record the maximum 'G', both positive and negative, reached during each flight; this was placed in the bombbay so that it could not be reset in flight! Altogether, this was an exciting time as the cockpit became more and more functional and businesslike.

All the systems were now finally installed and checked; we had fitted Avimo couplings into the hydraulic system so that we could test the operation using a ground-rig to supply pressure. The undercarriage retracted and extended with a satisfying 'clunk', the flaps went up and down as they should, the gills opened and closed smoothly, and the turret operated perfectly.

Using external power we could test and check all the electrics. We had installed a ground-charging point, extra filter and non-return valve, into the pneumatic system by the reservoir, so that it could be tested under pressure too.

The engines had been primed with oil and turned on the hand-cranks or starter motors (with the plugs out) until oil-pressure registered on the gauges. Fuel was put in the tanks and that system also was tested under pressure to ensure that there were no leaks.

The great day came on 10 July 1986 when the aircraft, still in yellow etch-primer and without the outer wings, was towed out and tethered down. It had been filled with pre-warmed oil, the felt pads in the rocker assemblies were soaked in warm oil, and the impellor bearings were primed.

Everything was ready to fire it up for the first time. The press had been informed. John Romain looked very harassed. We all kept our fingers crossed.

The starboard engine was turned through a couple of revolutions, the magnetos were switched on and it fired and ran instantly, giving the puff of white smoke characteristic of radial engines. A cheer rose from the small crowd present. We are sure that 'Chalky' was cheering too. It looked and sounded great. The team were very proud, and even the journalists were impressed. A series of checks and adjustments was followed by a programme of ground runs.

A few weeks later, following the same procedure, it was towed out again for the port engine to be started up. It turned over but wouldn't start. What an anticlimax! Investigation showed that when the magnetos had been removed for some other adjustment they had been put back with the ignition timing

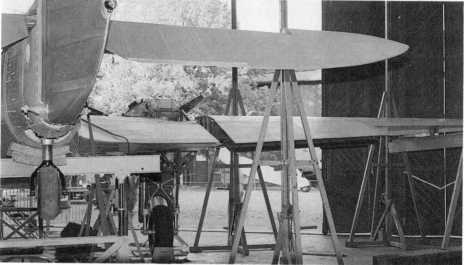

Top *Both engines running together for the first time in the airframe (still without the outer wings) — August 1986.*

Above *The starboard outer wing being attached to the airframe; the port outer wing followed several months later after the delays in rebuilding described in the text.*

Below *Work on the Blenheim often continued late into the night in a cold and draughty hangar.*

Another shot taken late at night, with John Gullick working on the starboard engine. A heat lamp was placed under each engine to reduce condensation in the unheated hangar.

Finally completed — the Blenheim airframe in yellow etch primer, with silver-doped control surfaces, is rolled out for the first time and stands by the Control Tower at Duxford in February 1987.

All eight bomb-doors in position; the centre ones hinge on the keel-plate, and the outer ones are not fully open. These were the last items fitted before the aircraft was painted.

out; when re-timed the engine started straight away and ran beautifully. It then followed the same programme as the other one until it reached the same point in the test schedule. Both engines could then be run together and the aircraft was fully alive at last. The programme of engine runs and tests continued and the results were all recorded.

The oil and filter was changed, the sump and pump filters checked. The oil pressure was set to 80 psi at 2,400 rpm. The fuel filters were cleaned, carburettor boost capsules checked and the linkages adjusted to give +4.5 lb supercharger pressure at take-off rpm. We had decided to restrict the engines to only half of the available +9 lb of boost, in the interests of engine longevity. This gave adequate performance as we operated the aircraft some 3,000 lb less than the maximum permissible in wartime conditions.

Our press release with photographs of the Blenheim with both engines running was widely publicized and many ex-Blenheim air and ground crews became aware of the rebuild for the first time and came to see it. The IWM started compiling a list of these ex-servicemen so that they could be invited to the first flight which was still a year away. This press release also contained a list of the Blenheim 'firsts' and background information on its important and gallant role in RAF service, and marked a milestone in our long campaign to make sure that it would no longer be the forgotten bomber.

Then it was back to the hangar where the engines were inhibited so that other work could continue. Over the winter, first the starboard wing was attached and then — quite a bit later — the port wing. The ailerons and outer flaps were fitted and tested. We had reinstated the landing lamp in the leading edge of the port wing (the Canadians used a retractable one) and new Perspex covers for the wing-tip lights were made and the lights fitted.

The remaining incomplete fairings and panels were made and fitted. All the control surfaces were carefully adjusted for the correct number of degrees movement in each direction. Everything was tightened, checked, split-pinned where needed, or locked, and signed-off. The pile of paperwork mounted higher and higher.

At last, in February 1987, we could tow out a complete Blenheim, looking strange in yellow etch-primer with silver-doped control surfaces. I say 'complete', but the bomb-doors were not quite ready.

Roy Pullan had made a full-sized jig and constructed an excellent working set of the eight folding doors, on curved wooden frames with marine-ply outer skins. They incorporated 'blisters' (originally to clear the bombs) and were hinged, in two sets of four, on the central keel plate and the outer sides of the bomb-bay. He is a good carpenter and did an excellent job on them.

A full rigging and dimensional symmetry check was then carried out. Measurements on each side from a point on each wing-tip to a point on the fin, and to one on the nose, were within ¼ in of each other; as they were from a point on the tailplane tips to the wing-tips and to a point on the fuselage. The distances from each tailplane tip to a bolt at the rear of each wheel-bay, and from the nose to the prop boss were also equal.

The fin was vertical, the tailplane horizontal, and the 6.5° dihedral on the outer wings and the 1° incidence angle of the wings were correct. The rudder moved 27.5° either side of the centre line, the elevators went up through 33° and down through 26°, the ailerons through 31° and 14° respectively, all exactly to design requirements. That this exceptionally accurate standard of reconstruction was achieved, considering the extremely derelict state of the original airframes before the restoration commenced, is a fine tribute to the skills of the team. Please bear in mind too that the centre section, main fuselage, keel-plate, and the outer wings, all originated from different airframes.

We were now ready to paint the aircraft in the chosen scheme and RAF markings.

It had been a long and difficult journey. Over 12 years and some 42,000 man-hours recorded in the work sheets (plus countless unrecorded hours) had been put into this unequalled restoration, together with quite a bit of money, but above all the unrivalled dedication and determination from the team. I say unequalled because I know of no other small, private, mainly volunteer team that has ever tackled — and completed successfully — such a major restoration of a complex wartime aircraft to so high a standard.

We now had the only flying Bristol Blenheim in the world!

Chapter Fifteen

Permit to fly

The aircraft was now de-greased all over, carefully masked up, and given two complete coats of a grey universal primer. The upper surfaces were then masked, and all the lower surfaces painted in the shade officially known as 'Sky' but unofficially as 'duck-egg blue'. Then they were masked off completely in turn and the upper surface painted in the correct 1941 scheme of Dark Earth and Dark Green to 'camouflage pattern A'.

We had researched the authentic colour scheme most carefully, assisted by the RAF museum at Hendon and by the expert K.B. Hiscock of Woodham Ferrers, using copies of original drawings supplied by the manufacturers.

The correct RAF markings of a 2 Group Bomber Command aircraft were applied, again carefully researched as to position, dimensions, style and actual colours. This applies also to the aircraft serial number V6028 and the Squadron letters 'G B' and the individual aircraft letter 'D Dog' of the 105 Squadron aircraft that we had chosen. These were the markings of the aircraft flown by Wing Commander Hugh Idwall Edwards DFC when he led the daylight attack on Bremen docks on 4 July 1941, for which operation he was awarded the Victoria Cross. These markings were chosen as 'Hughie' Edwards seemed to us to epitomize the unmatched bravery of the 'Blenheim Boys' that we wished to emphasize. He went on to become the most highest decorated serviceman of the Second World War and the most decorated Australian ever.

When the aircraft was towed out in April 1987, finally complete and resplendent in its 1941 colour scheme, it looked absolutely magnificent. Some had complained that it was slightly too 'shiny' and looked even better than brand new ones had! I must explain that we painted it in acrylic two-pack paint, as this is far more durable than cellulose; we used a matting agent so that it was not too glossy, but the dulling process had not had time to take effect and give that 'weathered' look.

Top *Both the aircraft and John are masked up well as he sprays on the grey filler-primer undercoats!*

Above *The right-hand cockpit seat showing the access steps, the cooling-gill controls above the map-case, the observer's round seat, and the throttles at the lower left.*

Below *The engines receive maintenance during the flight-test programme. This was the unexpected scene that so moved the New Zealand ex-Blenheim pilot.*

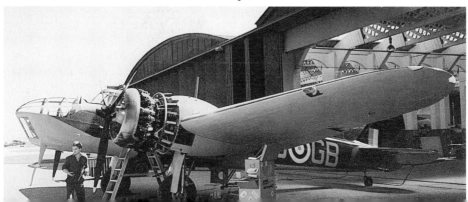

One touching incident demonstrated to us the strong evocative power of the Blenheim. An ex-Blenheim observer and gunner had met their wartime skipper again, a New Zealander on a visit to the UK, and brought him to Duxford without telling him what was in store. They walked him round a corner and there was the Blenheim, sitting between the hangars being worked on, a familiar sight during the war. The pilot was so overcome with emotion at this unexpected sight that he wept openly; clearly deep feelings and vivid memories were brought back.

The team worked even harder as the time for the long-awaited first flight drew near; the excitement was contagious, the enthusiasm more pronounced. The engines were prepared for action again, and full-power tests carried out.

The aircraft was weighed in the flying position, at 9,431 lb, the centre of gravity was measured, its fore and aft limits calculated, and a weight and balance schedule drawn up. Our chief pilot, John Larcombe, visited the CAA at Redhill and they agreed and approved a special flight-test programme that had to be concluded successfully before they could grant the permit to fly.

Taxiing trials commenced on 10 May. It was wonderful to see the aircraft moving under its own power at last. The speed in these taxi tests was increased progressively. The brakes had a most peculiar wailing sound when applied, that 'Roger Bacon' of *Flight* described as 'passable impersonations of peacocks in the mating season'.

The whole aircraft was checked, and then re-checked, all the systems were re-tested and cleared. Everything was signed off, the paperwork completed. The aircraft was passed 'fit for flight'. We were ready to go. John Larcombe, who was to be accompanied by John Romain as co-pilot and engineer, took time off from British Airways and was ready to go. Only the weather was not ready.

The aircraft was towed to the flight-line, started up and warmed up several times when the weather looked promising, but each time the drizzle and poor visibility returned to frustrate our efforts. The long-awaited first flight had to be postponed several times. Nerves were getting frayed.

At last, after yet another day of anxiously scanning dull skies and telephoning met offices, during the evening of 22 May, a weather 'window' opened just enough to allow the two Johns to 'go for it'.

The Blenheim was taxied to the end of Duxford's main runway, engine run ups and pre-take-off cockpit drills performed, the control tower gave 'clear to take off at your discretion' and it accelerated down the runway. We all held our breath.

The tail lifted — then the throttles were closed and it slowed to a stop. Our hearts missed a beat. Just as it had been about to lift off, there had been a loud noise and a rush of air, and John correctly aborted the take-off. The escape hatch under the nose had not been secured properly and had blown open! John Romain went down into the nose and secured it, then they taxied back to the other end of the runway.

Checks completed, the Blenheim accelerated again, once more the tail rose, then John lifted G-MKIV cleanly from the runway and suddenly it was airborne and climbing away with the wheels retracting. We all cheered.

More ground runs in the engine test programme — the cowlings are removed for better access.

John Larcombe with the Champagne carried on the first flight on 22 May 1987, which was 'cracked' after a remarkably trouble-free sortie.

John set cruising power, found it was perfectly rigged to fly straight and level, tried a few turns then did a couple of passes over the delighted team who were still out on the grass congratulating each other. We were surprised at its speed, its agility and the relative quietness of the Mercury engines. He came round and carried out a perfect landing.

We had done it — the world had an airworthy Blenheim once more.

John taxied in, it had started to rain once more but we scarcely noticed that. The champagne carried on the first flight was opened and passed round. It never tasted better! The team was euphoric.

The Blenheim was towed back to the hangar and sat there dripping, and tinkling quietly to itself as the engines cooled down. John said that it flew beautifully and that there were no snags to report. We repaired to the pub in Duxford village to celebrate. I for one could not really believe that we had actually done it. The whole flight still seemed unreal, like a fantasy.

However, it was real for the flight-test programme continued over the next few days. This included single-engined climbs, to establish minimum control speeds, etc with the landing gear both up and down. As the propeller of the 'failed' engine could not be feathered, it windmilled with the throttle closed thus creating considerable asymmetric drag, making this manoeuvre very demanding on both the pilot and the 'live' engine.

We noticed an oil-pressure reading on one engine that was lower than desired during these tests while it was working hard. This was worrying, but careful investigation showed it to be the indication on the electrical instrument. We added a pair of direct-reading gauges, mounted on the right of the panel angled towards the pilot, and the indicated pressures were then equal and normal. The only other problem of any significance was a low charging-rate which resulted in the batteries becoming discharged, but this was soon rectified.

Also when John was checking out Roy Pullan on the aircraft, Roy managed to get the hand-operated parking-brake on too firmly at the end of the runway, and pulled the nipple off the cable trying to release it, so that mission had to be abandoned for repairs to be carried out. Otherwise the aircraft was remarkably snag-free and proved a delight to fly.

John Larcombe submitted the official Flight Test Report to the CAA; their surveyor sent in his Airworthiness Approval Note (all 12 pages of it!) and the permit to fly was issued on 28 May, just in time for our 'official first flight' to which the press had been invited. Those ex-Blenheim crews who had left their names with the IWM over the preceeding years as they had watched the Blenheim taking shape were also invited along.

That day was fine and sunny. We had erected a marquee alongside the control tower, and provided refreshments and press packs. These contained not only information on the British Aerial Museum and the restoration team, but again listed the numerous 'firsts' and other achievements of Blenheims in RAF service.

The day was a great success; the ex-Blenheim people were delighted to be allowed to crawl all over it and many joyful reunions took place — one crew had not met up with each other since the war! We could see the years falling away

Top *John Larcombe makes a lovely low pass over Duxford on 29 May 1987.*

Above *A happy team with the FlyPast Trophy for the best aircraft restoration — 'Smudge' Smith, Nick Goodwyn, John Gullick, David and Colin Swann, John Romain, Hugh Smith, Chris Hollyer and David Smith. Billy was in the beer tent!* (IWM)

as memories of their Blenheim days were revived. One had flown in the original GB-D V6028 and showed us his logbook. We were glad to see 'Chalky's' widow, Pearl, there too.

John Larcombe started up the Blenheim, taxied out to clicking cameras, took off and gave a short, beautiful display. He approached first from behind the slight hill to the south of the airfield and held the Blenheim low towards the tower, pulling round in a tight turn, then performing several other graceful passes, before making his usual lovely three-point landing, and taxiing in to warm applause from those assembled.

We were pleased to have been voted the winners of the Mike Twite Trophy by the readers of *FlyPast* magazine for the best restoration, and it was presented alongside the Blenheim by Twite's widow. He had been the founder editor but was lost in an accident to a Vickers Varsity.

Later that afternoon John checked-out Roy on the Blenheim, and Roy did a sortie on his own. While this was going on we all rushed in to see the Blenheim featuring on both the BBC and ITV main new bulletins.

After the crowd had gone we sat together outside the marquee on that fine evening and enjoyed a few drinks, feeling very pleased with ourselves, and justifiably proud of our unique achievement.

That sunny afternoon was to me, and I believe to the rest of the team, the most memorable highlight of the entire Blenheim experience; an experience that we had shared together for so many years and through so many vicissitudes that it had become by then a major part of all our lives.

Chapter Sixteen

Return to the skies

While the flight-test programme was continuing, we had written to all the main airshow organizers giving details of the availability of this unique and exciting 'new' wartime aircraft on the air display scene. We also gave them some details of the RAF service, and many of the 'firsts' to the credit of the Blenheim, with our view of the Blenheim's long-neglected place in history. This was the beginning of our campaign to enlighten and inform the organizers and commentators, so that they in turn could start giving the facts about Blenheims to the public.

Although by June it was almost too late for the 1987 season because most display organizers book their participants many months ahead (and some didn't believe the Blenheim would be finished in time!), bookings were coming in fast. Those organizers that could not accommodate the Blenheim for 1987 wanted it for their 1988 displays. The income from these displays would start to recompense BAM for their very considerable expenditure. The future looked bright.

We were not ready for the Mildenhall Air Fete at the end of May, so the début for the Blenheim was to be at the Biggin Hill International Air Fair on 6 and 7 June, also taking part in events at Brands Hatch on the same weekend, and calling at Weathersfield for their open day on the way back. John Larcombe was to be the pilot for these five displays, assisted by John Romain.

The following weekend the Blenheim was the star at the big SSAFA Air Display at RAF Church Fenton in Yorkshire; the weekend after that (21 June) at the Duxford Military Display and at the Guild of Air Pilots and Air Navigator's Garden Party at Denham. The next weekend it was due at British Aerospace at Filton (the home of the Blenheim) for their open day, and at the Fighter Meet at North Weald. Roy Pullan was to fly the aircraft at these last four displays. Then in July it was due to be the 'warbird' star (and feature in

special BBC television coverage) at the huge International Air Tattoo at Fairford.

So it can be seen that we had a very busy season ahead of us — just at the events mentioned above the Blenheim would be seen in action 'live' by well over half a million people, and on television by millions more. It looked as if our aim of putting the Blenheim back on the map would soon succeed.

Richard Lucraft, the excellent PR man for Biggin Hill, asked us to take the Blenheim down there on 4 June, the Wednesday before the Air Fair, for a press and television reception to be held at Biggin on the Thursday to provide publicity both for the event and for the Blenheim. He had invited the national and local press, including both BBC and independent television and radio. We were delighted to accept, and as John Larcombe was off somewhere in a 747,

Far left *Graham Warner. A Shell photograph taken at the official first flight.*

Left *A delighted 'Smudge' after his first flight in the turret at Duxford.* (Photo by Mike Oakey of *Aeroplane Monthly*).

Below left *A girl in a 'Happiness is Big Bristols' T-shirt poses on a wartime motorcycle in front of the Blenheim. Happy days!*

Below *An evocative three-quarter rear shot of the Blenheim, with engines running and a 'Trolley-Acc' plugged in.*

I asked Roy Pullan if he would fly the Blenheim on this occasion, as well as the four displays mentioned above. He too was delighted.

Richard also had the bright idea of inviting Lord Rothermere to Biggin Hill on the Thursday and making a special presentation to him in recognition of the fact that his grandfather, the first Viscount Rothermere, had made the creation of the whole range of Blenheim aircraft possible in the first place. We prepared a mounted brass scale model of GB-D with a suitably engraved plaque. Richard had also invited Richard Passmore, the author of the book *Blenheim Boy* which describes very perceptively his experiences as a young Blenheim WOp/AG in the early days of the war.

I must explain at this juncture how it came about that John Larcombe and Roy Pullan were the only pilots who ever flew our Blenheim. Clearly the selection of pilots who could be entrusted with the Blenheim was absolutely crucial to the safe operation of this unique aircraft. Availability, suitability, experience on piston tailwheel aircraft, as well as display performances that I had observed over the years, were only some of the factors that had to be taken into consideration.

We had for many years insured our aircraft against third party liability and accidental loss, but our broker found it difficult to place the Blenheim at reasonable rates. Following his advice we in fact changed our insurance arrangements and the new underwriters would accept as named pilots only mature, suitably qualified and highly experienced pilots who were in current practice on multi-engined tail-wheel piston-engined aircraft.

Unfortunately this stipulation affected both John Romain, who I'm sure would have been an excellent pilot for it — for no one knows it better — and myself, for I would have loved to have flown the Blenheim. But we were ruled out as being insufficiently experienced for that aircraft, although we were covered for the others. Since then, John's experience has increased steadily — he flies The Fighter Collection's B25 Mitchell at displays — and he will be nominated to fly our second Blenheim.

John Larcombe is our chief pilot and had flown all the BAM piston-engined ex-military aircraft of both Robs Lamplough and myself for many years. He is an ex-RAF QFI, and was Officer i/c Standards at 4 FTS RAF Valley, where he monitored the performance of the instructors and trained many members of the Red Arrows. He is a very thorough pilot who doesn't get flustered in an emergency. He once suffered complete engine failure in Robs's Yak 11 whilst inverted at about 300 ft over Duxford in the middle of a 'hesitation roll' and carried out a successful forced-landing, and has what other pilots term 'a lovely pair of hands' in the smooth way he flies. He is currently a Training Captain with British Airways and is looking forward to flying the next Blenheim.

It is more difficult to be objective and impartial when talking of Roy Pullan, but I will try. He is a charming and erudite man with a delightful family, and is a genuine aircraft enthusiast. We enjoyed many pleasant social evenings together. As he was senior in both age and experience (with the latter gauged solely on the number of hours flown) to John, he felt that he should be the Chief Pilot. I explained that John had been with us longer and that he was my choice and I was unwilling to alter the position. Roy seemed to accept this, as he did when I resisted his request that he should carry out the first flight and testing of the Blenheim.

He had retired from British Airways as a Senior Captain, and was proud to have been with BOAC before that. He flew light twins a little for a small company, then he went back on 747s as a First Officer with Virgin Atlantic, but upon reaching 60 he finally had to retire from commercial flying. He had some 15,500 hours, had flown in the Harvard Formation Team, was current on our Beech 18, was being checked out on the B17 Fortress, and had never had an accident.

He had done a first class job on the moulds for the glazing and on the bomb-doors, as mentioned earlier. He helped to draw up the pilot's notes that we compiled from RAF, RCAF, Bristol and Fairchild Aircraft Co documents. So on paper he seemed ideal as a back-up pilot to John Larcombe for the Blenheim. Both men were acceptable as named Blenheim pilots to the underwriters.

A few warning bells had been rung over Roy's temperamental suitability but I failed to heed them. At the Goodwood Air Display the year before he had to abandon a take-off in the Beech 18 when he almost swung into a line of parked aircraft. He had failed to lock the tailwheel (the last vital action on lining up on the runway). I must accept part responsibility for that omission as I was in the right-hand seat and should have monitored his compliance with the cockpit drills. His display slot had been brought forward and he became flustered.

Similarly I must accept some responsibility for another near disaster that occurred the same weekend. Roy was in the middle of displaying the Beech 18 when I noticed the oil temperatures going right off the clock and the oil pressures rapidly sinking. He made an emergency call and landed immediately; the starboard engine seized as we taxied back.

He had opened the oil bypass valves, which provided for rapid warm up in the extremely cold conditions found in Canada by isolating the oil-cooler and main oil-tank, leaving just the oil in the engine in circulation. Again he was rushed and did his checks whilst taxiing out. He told me he was opening them, and simply forgot to close them and I failed to notice this — they are not in our check-list as we never used them. They should have been wired up. Fortunately, when the engines cooled down and we had changed the oil and filters no permanent damage was done, but it had been a close call.

There had been other examples of his forgetfulness at Duxford too, but I had given him the benefit of the doubt for there were extenuating circumstances. Once, after I had started and warmed up the Beech, he attempted to taxi it out with the pitot-cover still on, in heavy rain; and after a crewman signalled him to stop the port engine whilst he removed it, he was unable to restart the engine as he had left the mixture control in 'Lean'. And all this with a plane-load of passengers!

More seriously he had been reprimanded by the Safety Officer at a West Malling 'Great Warbirds' Meeting for flying low right over the pilot's tent on the crowd-line whilst displaying our Broussard in very poor weather

Above left *A fine air-to-air shot taken from the Beech 18 over Kent, showing the Blenheim's elegant but purposeful lines.*

Left *The gunner's view of Duxford airfield — the tailplane is at the top right!*

Above *The never-to-be-repeated formation at Biggin Hill.*

conditions. I was with him on this one too and we could see very little indeed, although I could see that one pass was a bit low and told him so. I did not accompany him when he was called to the Control Tower and he told me 'they had ticked him off gently for being on the low side'; I heard at an air display safety seminar later that his excuse was that 'he just couldn't see a thing and hadn't even noticed the tent'.

However, Roy was generally a very competent pilot, I believed that the heavy responsibility of being entrusted with flying the Blenheim would overcome such odd lapses of good airmanship, and his very occasional tendency to forgetfulness.

I briefed him as tactfully as I could on not allowing himself to become rushed, and the importance of always doing cockpit checks in one's own time, quoting similar errors I had made as examples. I briefed John Romain on this aspect too, knowing that he or I would be in the right-hand seat of the Blenheim, requesting him to take special care to monitor Roy's cockpit checks and procedures, as I would too.

However, back to Biggin Hill. I flew down with Roy in the Blenheim and he flew it by the book, performing a very good display for Lord Rothermere and the assembled press. He did several photo sorties for the press and television people, formating on the Beech which John Romain had brought down from Duxford.

We were delighted to see an excellent feature on the Blenheim in both the midday and evening television news programmes, Michael Sullivan's piece for the BBC being very good indeed.

Capital Radio did a live 'The way it is' broadcast from the Blenheim too. Richard Passmore went up in the turret — the first time he had been in one since his wartime Blenheim crashed and he was taken prisoner — and the *Evening Standard* did an absorbing feature on this. Most of the nationals covered the event as well, and Richard Lucraft was very pleased with the coverage.

One of the most rewarding aspects of the day was seeing the look of keen delight on the faces of the ex-Blenheim crew whilst they inspected the Blenheim on the Biggin apron and watched the short display. The pleasure they gained from greeting old comrades and seeing a Blenheim in the air once more showed in their animated and joyful manner.

Apart from one heavy landing, the only difficulty Roy had was when he had to pull the Blenheim off the taxiway on to the grass and stop the engines, to avoid running into the tail of the Beech. It had been a lengthy downhill and downwind taxi on a warm day and we believe that he experienced brake-fade in the drum-braked Blenheim behind the disc-braked Beech, for when it had all cooled down the loss of braking effect was no longer apparent.

Lord Rothermere thoroughly enjoyed his visit and stayed far longer than scheduled. He studied our photo album of the restoration and was delighted with his presentation Blenheim, and even climbed into the cockpit of the real one. Richard Lucraft was nervous lest he should slip on the wing and fall, because it is a steep climb up to the hatch above the cockpit and very hard on the way down to locate the foot-holds inserted in the sides of the port fuselage by the trailing edge. He was charming to the team members and ex-Blenheim crew that he met there too, and the *Daily Mail* gave the event a good report with illustrations.

It was a very good day and the Blenheim had basked in both sunshine and glory, and the fact that one was flying again after so many years was seen by millions. We put it in a hangar and went back to Duxford in the Beech that evening very pleased with ourselves.

We returned to Biggin in the Beech, and Roy brought the Broussard down with some friends because he had to return and display it at Duxford on the Sunday. The Blenheim was much admired on the flight-line and the crowd witnessed its first public display, flown by John Larcombe with John Romain in the right seat.

It performed perfectly on a bright but very windy day, and took part in a unique Second World War formation with a Mosquito flown by George Aird and the B17 *Sally B* flown by Keith Sissons; a fine sight sadly never to be repeated as the Mosquito left for the United States soon after, and the Blenheim was to crash just two weeks later.

The two Johns performed their other four displays that weekend as scheduled with no problems at all, but returned straight to Duxford, as the crosswind affecting the Biggin Hill runway was getting stronger.

Our busy air display season had started off in fine style. The Blenheim created great interest, was much admired, constantly photographed, and had performed faultlessly throughout. The aircraft logbook shows that from 8 to 10 June a full post-permit check was carried out on the aircraft; all the filters were cleaned and inspected, brake-pressure adjusted to 60 psi per side, the main oleo pressures adjusted to 365 psi, and the engine idling set at 650 rpm. Everything was thoroughly inspected, checked and found satisfactory.

The next weekend John Larcome took the Blenheim to Church Fenton, where it had star billing in the SSAFA Display, but unfortunately the weather was very poor indeed. It needed all his skill to get it there and back safely in the awful conditions, and to give what was by all accounts a fine display.

He was not to know that he would never be able to fly that Blenheim again. For the next Sunday was 21 June 1987.

Chapter Seventeen

Shattered dreams

Sunday 21 June 1987 — a date never to be forgotten by any of the Blenheim team. We had arranged to demonstrate the Blenheim on that day at the Guild of Air Pilots and Air Navigators Garden Party at Denham Airfield, which included a select air display, and also at the Duxford Military Display on the same afternoon.

The GAPAN event, a private function not open to the public, is attended by everyone who is anyone in the aviation world. We were going as a favour to the organizers of the air display, two British Airways captains known to John Larcombe, and at a purely nominal fee. It is necessary to give the complete background to this air display at Denham for it has a vital bearing on the disaster that followed.

The organizers asked if it might be possible for the Blenheim to land in the morning, before Denham was closed to normal traffic, as they would quite like it to be on static display prior to carrying out its aerial demonstration and leaving for Duxford. I said that although we would look into the possibility, I very much doubted if it would be feasible owing to the small size of Denham airfield. They understood my reservations and did not attempt any persuasion.

Roy was informed of the query and of my reservations, as it would be his decision as captain. I did not influence this purely operational decision (nor have I ever attempted to influence an operational decision of any pilot) or bring even the slightest pressure to bear, one way or the other, except to emphasize that 'the safety of the aircraft must be paramount'.

Thus if the weather for any sortie looked doubtful, a snag that affected the aircraft's serviceability arose, or the crosswind on the runway was nearing limits (to give but a few examples), it was always the captain's responsibility to decide whether to attempt that particular flight or not. Only he is in a position to make that type of operational decision and it would be quite wrong of me to attempt to influence or override it, even if I were there — which of course frequently I was not.

Before the event it was agreed that we would not land at Denham, not only because the available runway length was marginal, but also because we had not been operating the Blenheim long enough to determine its normal landing and take-off performance, yet alone its short landing and take-off capabilities.

It is possible that by the end of the year, with far more time on the aircraft to enable us to establish these crucial parameters, and to familiarize both pilots with the handling techniques required, plus ample practice in such demanding manoeuvres on a larger airfield, the aircraft may have been able to land and take off from Denham quite safely. But at that very early stage of our operations on the Blenheim sound airmanship dictated that it would be unwise and unsafe to attempt to do so.

Therefore, when Roy informed me that he had decided not to land at Denham I agreed fully with his decision and told him that it was certainly the correct one, and asked him to advise the organizers of this decision. Another factor which may have influenced him was that, if he had wanted to be at Denham in the morning he would have had to leave home very early in order to drive to Duxford in time to fly to Denham. Also there were ground events at Duxford in the morning and he would have to leave before they started.

Consequently both display organizers were informed by Roy that we would not be landing at Denham. So it was arranged that we would take off from Duxford at the conclusion of the ground events, fly to Denham and do the demonstration without landing, and return to Duxford to fly straight into the display 'slot' there, landing afterwards at the end of the whole sortie.

The times of the display slots at each event, which are all timed to the half-minute, were carefully co-ordinated by both organizers to allow for this, and the display programmes at both events were finalized on this basis.

I intended to go with Roy in the right-hand seat of the Blenheim that day as co-pilot and engineer, as it was a CAA stipulation that it be occupied by a qualified co-pilot with a knowledge of the aircraft, so it had to be either John Romain or myself if John Larcombe was not available. That would have been an enjoyable trip for me, as it was the main item at the Duxford Military Air Display and the Blenheim was making its long awaited début at a public display there. However, the guest of honour at Duxford was HRH Prince Michael of Kent and it was arranged that I would be presented, so I had to forgo my trip in the Blenheim.

I often wonder how things would have turned out had I accompanied Roy.

Would I have overridden him when he announced at the end of his display that he was going to do a 'touch and go' landing, and forbidden it? That would certainly have led to a row in the cockpit, which is not a good thing during a display, and undoubtedly would have affected his performance at Duxford, possibly dangerously so. For these reasons I may have said nothing, intending to discuss it after we had landed back at Duxford.

Had I remained in the cockpit and the accident happened as it did I would most probably have been killed, for I am not as young or fit as John Romain and he was thrown out right through the roof. Would Roy even have attempted a landing with me alongside him, knowing that we had agreed not to?

I asked John Romain to go when I heard, about 10 days before, that I was required to stay at Duxford. John was not very happy as he did not share my confidence in Roy's flying, He had heard that Roy had been considering landing at Denham and was firmly against this, particularly as John Larcombe had said that *he* would not attempt to do so at that early stage of our operation of the Blenheim.

Indeed John Romain felt so strongly on the matter that he told me he was not prepared to fly with Roy if he intended to land there, although Roy was unaware of this. It posed a dilemma for me as it would probably have led to the cancellation of the Denham sortie. So I was very relieved when Roy told me that he had decided not to attempt a landing there for, unknown to him, it resolved that dilemma, and John was pleased when I told him of Roy's decision.

The aircraft had been checked over thoroughly during the week, and was started up, warmed up and tested on the Sunday morning. It was running beautifully, and was parked at the eastern end of the Duxford flight-line next to the RAF Lancaster.

John Romain had asked 'Smudger' Smith to go as the third crew member. I saw Roy briefly in the crew-room and we discussed the weather, which was good, and checked the timing of flying straight into his two display slots at the appropriate times. For Duxford it was intended to make a fast, low, curving entry from behind the hangars at the western end of the airfield, which would have been a dramatic début. My last words to him were, 'Enjoy yourself Roy, but do look after it.'

The Blenheim started at the correct time, with the usual brief cloud of white oil-smoke from radial engines that had stood for a few hours since the morning running. Roy taxied out and carried out full-power ground tests on each engine, assisted by John Romain, as part of the pre-take-off checks. All was exactly as it should have been. He took off on the main 24 runway, then came round and did one pass before departing to the west. The Blenheim looked absolutely beautiful in the sunshine. We awaited its return with eager anticipation.

At Duxford the time for the appearance of the Blenheim drew near, I looked out — ever more anxiously — to the west expecting to see it holding. The time passed. It did not appear. A Harvard took its place in the programme. I knew that something unplanned and untoward had taken place. I convinced myself that it must have landed at Denham with some minor mechanical problem which was being sorted out. I was called to the control tower over the PA. As I walked along in front of the crowd-line I feared that something must be seriously wrong, but was quite unprepared for the stunning news I received.

In the tower I was told by Mervyn Fortune, the Air Traffic Controller, that the Blenheim had crashed badly at Denham. He understood that the crew had survived but were injured and were being taken to hospital.

It took some while to establish by telephone which hospitals they had been taken to, and then, thankfully, that their injuries were not critical. Both Roy's wife Sheila and his daughter Anna, as well as John's wife Amanda and my wife Shirley, were in the tower during this very distressing period. The team were dumbfounded and deeply shocked. As soon as we knew which hospitals were involved I left for them with Shirley, as we were both deeply concerned for the crew.

At the Hillingdon Hospital we saw the two Johns, both very pale, clearly shaken, badly bruised, and well bandaged up. Little John had painful injuries to his right shoulder and elbow, plus head injuries and concussion, resulting from his ejection through the cockpit canopy.

Both John and 'Smudger' had seen the accident coming; John could do nothing about it — his ever more urgent warnings to the pilot had no effect — but 'Smudger' had taken up a protective position by the main spar and was

The port engine, torn off in the accident and laying behind the starboard wing. (Flypast)

bounced around heavily inside the fuselage. He was badly bruised and had various cuts and abrasions. He told me that they had landed, swung off the runway, tried to overshoot, climbed up again and crashed on to Denham Golf Course. The aircraft had cartwheeled over, the back was broken, and both engines had been completely torn off. Most fortunately there had been no fire and the emergency services had been there 'in less than two minutes'.

He said that Roy had offered, via the radio to Denham Tower, to perform a 'touch and go before departing to Duxford' after they had thanked him on completion of his display; and that John Romain had queried the need for this unexpected extra manoeuvre but was overruled by the captain.

At the High Wycombe Hospital we found that Roy was unconscious, he looked deathly pale, his head and face were heavily bandaged and he was connected to various drips and drains. We were told that his condition was serious but not critical. We were unable to speak to him, but asked Sheila to concentrate on his recovery for neither of them was to worry over possible causes of the accident.

As I said to her, and to many friends and relatives of the crew, plus all of our team members: 'The most important thing, that we must be thankful for, was that no one was killed or severely injured, for aeroplanes can be rebuilt but human beings are irreplaceable.'

We left the hospital and went to Denham Golf Course. By then it was a dull and drizzly evening which deepened our depression further. We saw the poor Blenheim laying there twisted and torn. The port engine was behind the starboard wing; the fuselage was broken in half at the turret, the entire nose had just vanished. Some of the team were gathering bits and pieces. They were shattered and some were in tears. All of them had put so much effort over so many years into re-creating the only flying Blenheim in existence that they were at that stage severely shocked and quite inconsolable. It was clear that the aircraft was damaged far too badly ever to be rebuilt. We realized just what an astonishing miracle it had been that none of the crew or any person on the ground had been killed.

I was appalled to learn that Roy had been attempting a 'touch and go' landing and had 'got it all wrong' when he crashed the aircraft. I must explain that this term is short for 'touch down and go round again' and is essentially a training manoeuvre comprising a normal landing following which, instead of bringing the aircraft to rest on the runway, the pilot immediately applies (or calls for) full power and takes off or 'goes round again'. It is used mainly to avoid prolonged taxiing between practice circuits and landings, and is not a recognized air display manoeuvre.

If Roy had mentioned his intention before the event to perform one, or asked my permission to do so, I certainly would have prohibited it.

I thought Roy had made the disastrous decision to attempt one entirely on the spur of the moment; he claimed later to have 'planned the whole manoeuvre carefully in advance', and that he was 'convinced he could do it safely as he had done it thousands of times before'.

But he had not even tried one before in the Blenheim, even though he had

had ample opportunity to do so at Biggin Hill and Duxford, which both have nice long runways. His experience on handling the Blenheim was very limited indeed, and he knew the length of the runway at Denham was, at best, marginal. Who can say why he did it?

When I asked John Larcombe, after Roy's check flight on the Blenheim, how it had gone, he said that Roy gave the impression that he felt the check wasn't really necessary, and showed some impatience when John was 'showing him the ropes'. On pressing him if he considered that Roy was safe to fly the aircraft he said, 'Yes he was, as long as he didn't get a rush of blood to the head.'

The trouble was that he did, for something caused him to abandon all good airmanship and attempt this very unwise and, in the circumstances, highly dangerous manoeuvre. He seemed not to take into account that he had not even practised one on the Blenheim, yet alone rehearsed it as part of the display sequence. For it is a golden rule at air displays that only adequately practised manoeuvres are included in a properly planned air display, the entire programme then being rehearsed thoroughly beforehand.

He ignored the fact that Denham, in the course of an air display, was a most unsuitable place to try such a demanding manoeuvre in the Blenheim for the very first time. He dismissed the objections of his co-pilot. He discounted the high degree of risk to which this manoeuvre would expose a unique part of our aviation heritage. It would seem that he did not even consider the potential danger to the very lives of his fellow crewmen. He disregarded completely all normal, prudent and responsible considerations.

The team believe that his sound judgement in the safe conduct of the display was cast aside because he was determined to demonstrate a 'touch and go' landing there and then. They feel that the Blenheim was needlessly sacrificed on the altar of his ego. Unfortunately I can find no other explanation that fits all the known facts for his grossly irresponsible behaviour that day, although it grieves me to record such a sad commentary on human nature.

Both 'Smudger' and John Romain were innocent parties who were very lucky indeed not to have been killed or seriously injured in the accident. Had either of them been, we would not have wished to continue the second restoration and the memory of the flying Blenheim eventually would have faded away, so that their survival is a miracle that we all should be thankful for on both counts.

It should be explained that on the Blenheim's primative hydraulic system, which was virtually the first in any RAF aircraft, a master control in the cockpit has to be selected from the neutral 'off' position to either 'flaps and undercarriage' or 'turret' to pressurize the circuit required; selecting either position cuts off all hydraulic power to the other. During the display at Denham the pilot selected the former as he wanted partial flap and the undercarriage lowered to perform a slow flypast before his ill-fated attempt at a 'touch and go' manoeuvre, but he did not warn the occupant of the turret that the power was about to be turned off, as he had been briefed to do. Fortunately for 'Smudger' he had the guns pointed towards the tail and upwards, which lowers the seat, at the very moment the power was disconnected and he was just able to extricate himself from the turret, for it is very cramped and he is a large man.

Had he been unable to do so he would almost certainly been killed for, as the Blenheim cartwheeled on to the golf course the fuselage broke its back at the turret which was severely compressed. Indeed the breech-blocks of the pair of Browning .303 machine-guns were forced forward so that they were almost touching the front of the remains of the turret mounting ring around the seat where 'Smudger' had been sitting moments before. As it was he curled up inside the fuselage and was thrown around, in his own words, 'like a pea in a pod'.

Naturally I sympathize with fellow pilots whom the press brand as guilty of 'pilot error' before the facts concerning an aircraft accident are established — it is all too easy a conclusion to reach, and often difficult to disprove. In this widely publicized accident, however, the aircraft was blamed. Several press reports stated that the aircraft 'suffered engine failure' or 'had engine trouble', another 'that it was seen to stream fuel before it crashed' so that members of the public had been informed that the aircraft had a mechanical failure and therefore was not properly airworthy. This casts doubts on the integrity and workmanship of the restoration team. It was suggested that such historic aircraft are not safe and should not be allowed to fly.

It is necessary therefore to set the record straight, to record that the aircraft was perfect mechanically and fully airworthy, and to emphasize the sole culpability of the pilot, in order to clear the name of the restoration team and the operators of this historic aircraft.

Some have said 'He will have this on his conscience for the rest of his life, leave him in peace' but he seems convinced that it was not his fault. He has publicly stated that 'it was a perfectly proper manoeuvre' that he 'would have carried it out safely' and had 'done it thousands of times before' and apparently is still trying to convince others that the fault lies with the aircraft and not with him.

However, I cannot avoid the fact that the ultimate responsibility for the accident must rest squarely on my own shoulders for it was I who entrusted this unique aircraft to the pilots who flew it, as after that it was literally in their hands not mine, although I feel that I took all reasonable precautions to make sure that the pilots selected were each capable and worthy of that trust.

With regard to a description of what took place in the cockpit on that last flight and a factual analysis of the series of misjudgements and final gross mishandling of the aircraft that led to the crash, with details of the accident itself, I feel it best to reproduce a letter that I wrote to Roy soon after the event, which sets them out fully and as accurately as possible. (See Appendix 4.) Subsequent events have substantiated its veracity entirely.

The report of the Senior Accident Inspector, Department of Transport Accident Investigation Branch, is also reproduced. (See Appendix 3.) Most unusually it states:

'The operating company had taken great pains to ensure that the aircraft was fully airworthy and that the pilot was capable of safely performing the display.'

Chapter Eighteen

'A Blenheim will fly again'

The reaction when I returned home on the night of the accident made life very hectic. I was drained both mentally and physically, and wanted only to flop into bed, but the telephone didn't stop ringing all night (and I am ex-directory), so by 3 am I took it off the hook. Someone at Denham had told the enquiring press reporters that the aircraft had suffered an engine failure on take-off.

Earlier that night I rang Richard Lucraft and agreed a press statement with him. We played down the accident as much as possible and said that the Blenheim had force-landed on the golf course, the crew had only suffered minor injuries, the cause was unknown but the AIB were investigating and would report their findings in due course. Most of the responsible papers carried this statement, many with photographs of the stricken aircraft.

We went to see John and Roy again in hospital a couple of days later; 'Smudger' had been released and John soon would be, though his injuries troubled him for some time. Roy was recovering well, but had trouble with his nose, though he was asleep when we called to see him so we still had not spoken.

The accident received widespread coverage in the national press, and on the television news. The Blenheim had certainly hit the headlines but not in the way we wanted! The calls continued to flood in, as they did to the IWM at Duxford and to *FlyPast* and *Aeroplane* magazines too, but the calls were less outraged and far more sympathetic.

Some had said that 'such historic aircraft should not be allowed to fly' and blamed us for its destruction. I must make my view on this clear: if there is only one surviving example of an airframe in existence then I would agree that it would be most unwise for it to be allowed to fly. However, if more than one example exists then I believe that as many people as possible should be given

the opportunity to see the type in action in the air, where it belongs. Static
aircraft exhibited in museums do not have the same magical appeal as a live one
performing in its true element — the sky.

A mass of letters arrived at Duxford and at my home, many from ex-
Blenheim air or ground-crew who had been deeply shocked to hear of its loss
and offered to help in any way they could. Many sent unsolicited cheques for
small amounts. Most begged us to rebuild it if we could, or to 'find another
one' as 'the Blenheim must not be allowed to fade away again'.

I received handwritten personal letters from Lord Rothermere, who was very
supportive; from Air Chief Marshal Sir Wallace Kyle (President of the RAF 2
Group Association), known as 'Digger' in his Blenheim days when he was
Hughie Edwards's Squadron then Base Commander; and Air Marshall Sir Ivor
Broom, another distinguished ex-Blenheim pilot (KCB, CBE, DSO and two
bars, DFC and bar, AFC, etc) Chairman of the Royal Air Force Association.
They all urged me not to let go to waste all that we had achieved and learnt on
restoring the first Blenheim to fly, but to put one back in the air if it was at all
possible.

This response was so overwhelming — within the week we had received
hundreds of telephone calls and some 1,200 letters — that I realized that we
really had no alternative — it just had to be done all over again.

Therefore I contacted each member of the team in person to ask them what
they thought about this very daunting prospect. I would not have blamed
them if they never wanted anything to do with Blenheims again. Quite
extraordinarily, every single one was more than willing to restore another
Blenheim to flying condition, despite what they had just gone through. They
said 'You get the airframe and we will make it fly', or 'We've done it once so
we can do it again', or 'If you can supply the hardware we can put it together'.
I found their loyalty and dedication to the Blenheim cause was even stronger
than it had been before. So I asked Richard to arrange a press conference at
Duxford for the following Monday, just a week after news of the accident had
appeared.

We collected the crashed aircraft from Denham. Peter Paige of the Duxford
Aviation Society was particularly helpful in arranging this sad task, and laid out
the broken and twisted remains in the hangar. The team found this to be both
disturbing and depressing. Richard and I had put together a press pack with
photographs, and he issued the invitations.

So many people had written and sent unsolicited amounts that I decided to
open a Blenheim appeal fund to help finance the second restoration.

I was shattered not only by the accident and the near loss of close friends, but
also by the destruction of all our high hopes and exciting future plans for the
Blenheim. I was disturbed by the knowledge that we had been denied the
substantial income from air displays that, after a few seasons, would have
returned my heavy personal investment. I knew that I was not able to back a
second restoration entirely from my own pocket, and if it was to be done then
the appeal fund was essential.

We had a good turn-out of national, local and aviation press, plus BBC and independent television crews.

Ted Inman, the Keeper at Duxford, introduced me to them saying that as an exhibit the Blenheim 'was the jewel in the crown at Duxford' and offering to provide the facilities as before to assist in another Blenheim rebuild. I informed the press conference that we were going to take on this second restoration of a Blenheim to flying condition, and that we aimed to complete it in five years, rather than the 12 that the first one had taken. I paid public tribute to the whole team and especially to John Romain.

I announced the launching of The Blenheim Appeal with the slogan 'A Blenheim will fly again', and explained that the more support we received the sooner the second restoration would be completed. I said that we had the ability and expertise, the facilities and the determination, but needed financial support to help us succeed. Our intention to form a Blenheim Society for supporters of the second restoration, with a newsletter to keep them in touch with progress on it, was made public.

The three Johns — Romain, Larcombe and Smith — were all interviewed by the press and television, as was I, and we received very good coverage.

The die was cast! The Blenheim team was committed to starting the whole lengthy and difficult process all over again.

The announcement of The Blenheim Appeal was carried by all the aviation magazines, with but one exception, and by the *Daily Mail*, *Sunday Express*, *Mail on Sunday* and *Evening Standard*. Donations, many from ex-Blenheim personnel, and letters offering support, arrived in increasing numbers. Each one was acknowledged personally. An example of this Blenheim Appeal announcement is reproduced as Appendix 5, which explains exactly what we are trying to do, and why we are doing it.

Blenheim-related merchandise was organized, largely by Andy Gilmour of The New Granary Print and Design unit at Linton, assisted by Marianne Larcombe with other friends and relatives, and sold with the proceeds going to the Blenheim Appeal. The most popular item, thought up by 'Smudger,' was a T-shirt with a picture of two Mercury radial engines and the slogan 'Happiness is Big Bristols' in the appropriate place on the front! Our own video of the first Blenheim restoration was put together by 'Smudger' and some of his colleagues, and marketed by DD Video Distributors.

Richard Lucraft specially commissioned and published two beautiful Blenheim limited edition prints, from originals painted by the renowned aviation artists Frank Wootton and Gerald Coulson. These were most successful and contributed very significantly to The Blenheim Appeal. When a Blenheim does take to the skies once more it will be due largely to the efforts of enthusiasts like Richard, Andy, and all those who have supported the appeal so generously.

The Team would like to express sincere thanks for this wonderful level of support, which they find most encouraging, for they know that they cannot succeed without it.

In the meantime I had to deal with the Civil Aviation Authority, who carried out a thorough investigation into the airworthiness and operational aspects of the aircraft and the accident. They later exonerated us completely as operators. Our insurance broker, Norman Pocock, did his best to assist but it was left to me to deal at length with Lloyd's Aviation Department's senior surveyor and loss adjustor, who were anxious to establish the causes of the accident to see if we as owners and operators were in any way responsible, as this could have reduced or removed their liability.

I had to deal too with the Accident Investigation Branch of the Ministry of Transport, who were conducting the official investigation into the safety aspects of the accident.

All these dealings were complicated by Roy Pullan's attitude as, although he had no recollection whatsoever of the accident, he objected to the AIB draft report, and it was twice revised to be far less critical of his actions as the pilot responsible. The insurance company would not settle the claim until this and the CAA investigation were concluded. Roy was trying to avoid any responsibility for the accident being attributed to him by attempting to blame anyone and anything but himself. The team would have some respect for him if he had been man enough to say that he was sorry.

I feel that he cannot admit, even to himself, that he caused the accident. He seems convinced that the team have conspired to blame him. Perhaps his mind refuses to accept the fact that the responsibility is his and his alone. If so, it is a tragedy for his family, who naturally support him through loyalty, but also most unfair on the team.

In January 1989 Roy Pullan was prosecuted by the Civil Aviation Authority and tried on two criminal charges under Articles 47 and 48 of the Air Navigation Orders. They were 'A person shall not recklessly or negligently act in a manner likely to endanger an aircraft or the persons therein' and 'A person shall not recklessly or negligently cause an aircraft to endanger any person or property' and are the most serious charges a pilot can face.

The case commenced on Monday 16 January and was bitterly contested throughout by Pullan's QC. Those members of the team summoned as witnesses, including myself, found it an uncomfortable and draining experience which brought it all back to us all too vividly.

On Friday 27 January he was convicted on both charges, fined £1,000 on each, and ordered to make a substantial contribution to the prosecution costs. That long, sad and wearying chapter was finally closed. At last we could look ahead to the next Blenheim and put the loss of the first one behind us.

Many ex-Blenheim air and ground crew, and many more who had lost relatives on Blenheims, plus very many ordinary Blenheim supporters who subscribed to the appeal, had asked if we could form a 'Friends of the Blenheim' Association or Supporters' Club for the Blenheim, and more enquiries as to this were received when we announced at the press conference on 29 June that we were forming a Blenheim Society.

Before our first Blenheim flew I had been the guest of honour at the annual dinner of the 2 Group RAF Officer's Association and was invited to address this most distinguished gathering on the restoration of the Blenheim. As the principal operators of Blenheims in the thick of the wartime action they were most interested in the project and delighted that one would fly again and at last receive the recognition it deserved. I was also invited to a reunion dinner at Huntingdon on 4 September 1989 by some ex-2 Group people. This followed a visit they had made to RAF Wyton where we had been due to take the Blenheim on 3 September to commemorate the outbreak of the Second World War, but of course the accident prevented this.

These ex-service people too were talking about the possibility of forming a Blenheim Association, as our airworthy Blenheim and its terrible accident had received such widespread publicity that it acted as a catalyst to many ex-Blenheim types to get together and see what they could do to help.

An *ad hoc* committee was elected, or should I say press ganged, from the diners that night, with Betty George, the leading light behind the reunion dinner, as Honorary Secretary — and a very diligent one she turned out to be! The Chair was offered to me but I had to decline owing to my heavy commitments, and Betty's husband Wing Commander 'Hugh' George (an ex-XV Squadron Blenheim pilot) stepped into the breach and assumed that responsibility.

We held an immediate committee meeting in the early hours, and agreed that as our aims coincided we should get together to form a suitable association, for it would be silly to have two such Blenheim-related bodies. So The Blenheim Society was formed there and then and resolved to adopt the following objectives:

a) To raise funds and offer expertise to assist in restoring the British Aerial Museum's Blenheim to flying condition.
b) To retrieve and record the true history of the Blenheim and its air and ground crews in RAF service.
c) To organize functions and events for reunions of veterans of the Blenheim squadrons and others interested in the aircraft.

I should mention that the committee agreed to pursue all three aims equally and they are set out in no particular order. Though clearly the ex-servicemen (and women) had a greater interest in the second and third aims above, and my main concern was the first one, I supported the other two just as whole-heartedly, as it was all helping the good cause of the Blenheim.

An inaugural function for the Blenheim Society was arranged as a buffet lunch in the Officer's Mess at Duxford, and I contacted as many as possible of the ex-Blenheim people who had written to me or subscribed to The Blenheim Appeal, as possible. Over 300 turned up on a very foggy November day and The Blenheim Society was off to a flying start.

There are now over 600 members and it is growing all the time. An excellent, informative and well-illustrated *Blenheim Journal* (edited by Norman McLeod, a serving RAF Squadron Leader) is sent free to all members. It contains many fascinating features and through it I can keep Society Members informed and up to date on the progress of the second restoration.

The Blenheim Society archivist, Hugh Wheeler, is busy gathering

information both from official sources, such as squadron histories or
operational records (which are often scant or inaccurate) and from the personal
recollections of survivors, so that the true and full history of the valiant wartime
service of the Blenheim may be published.

I put in hand the production of a one-hour documentary of the Blenheim in
RAF service, which was made by Barry Heard and his Freeze Frame Production
Company. Introduced by Lord Rothermere, it contains much interesting
archive film from *Britain First* to wartime Blenheims in action, and our
restoration and the accident, plus some fascinating interviews with Blenheim
survivors. I was happy to act as historical adviser to this production, along with
Air Commodore 'Ted' Sismore, a highly regarded 2 Group Blenheim and
Mosquito man. Called *The Forgotten Bomber* it was first shown by Anglia
Television, but has now been taken up by Central, Grampian, HTV and some
other regions. We have put the Blenheim and some of the deeds of the brave
Blenheim Boys in front of several million people: no longer can it be called 'the
forgotten bomber'!

The insurance complications were finally resolved and·we received settlement
just before Christmas, having negotiated to purchase the salvage of the wrecked
aircraft from the insurance company so that we could utilize any parts from it
that may help the next rebuild. Unfortunately it could not be insured for its
probable full open market value, as the premiums would have become
prohibitive, and it is very hard to determine and then agree with the insurers
the real value of the only airworthy example of such an historic aircraft in the
world. In the eyes of the team it was priceless anyway!

Ironically, we had virtually concluded negotiations for commercial sponsorship of these expensive insurance costs, which would have enabled us to
increase the amount of cover obtained to a higher and possibly more realistic
value, when the aircraft was destroyed and it was too late.

After compiling a complete list of all the known Bristol Type 149 Blenheim/
Bolingbroke airframes in the world, and carefully assessing their suitability and
availability, we selected and purchased the best that we could find. This
replacement airframe and other components, including two engines, were
delivered to Duxford in February 1988; it comprised the main parts of RCAF
10201 — like the first, a derelict Canadian hulk — with the wings of 9703.

As one member of the team said, 'It's like being at the foot of Everest all over
again.'

I am pleased to advise that to date we are on target to complete the second
restoration within the five-year timescale we set ourselves, so that once more
the world will be able to see an airworthy Bristol Blenheim.

For we are all very determined that 'A Blenheim will fly again'!

Flight test reports

CIVIL AVIATION AUTHORITY

AIRWORTHINESS DIVISION

Ftce.

Airworthiness
Flight Test Schedule No.3
Issue 1
March 1976.

TWIN, PISTON-ENGINED UN-PRESSURIZED AEROPLANES
UP TO 5700 kg. (12,500 lb) MAW

1. INTRODUCTION

This Schedule applies to the aeroplane types listed in the Appendix. Where a
type is not listed, or where an air test is required to clear a Modification,
appropriate schedules will be agreed between the Applicant and the CAA.

The Schedule is written on the assumption that the pilot understands, and will
follow the instructions and advice in, CAA leaflet "Pilot Briefing on
Airworthiness Flight Testing of Light Aeroplanes Issue 2".

It is recommended that the tests are made in the sequence given. The results
are to be written in ink in the spaces provided. Write YES/NO or SAT/UNSAT.
or appropriate words. Do not use ticks or crosses.

2. GENERAL

The aeroplane and its engines are at all times to be operated within the limitations imposed by the Certificate of Airworthiness (C of A), by cockpit placards
and instrument colour coding, and by the Flight Manual. Aeroplanes for which
there is no approved Flight Manual must be flown to the limitations in the
appropriate Manual designated on the C of A. The normal operating checks and
drills given in the Manual must be followed.

An observer should be carried to record the results of the tests.

In accordance with Aeronautical Information Circular 126/1972, an engine should
not be deliberately shut down at an altitude less than 3,000 feet above terrain,
for the purposes of these flight tests.

During the flight test, the crew must monitor the behaviour of all equipment
and report any unserviceable items. In particular, if the test flight follows
maintenance work, it is important to make sure that the items involved function
satisfactorily, and that no additional faults have accidentally resulted.

Operator/Maintenance Organization	BRITISH AERIAL MUSEUM	Flight Test Report	No.	1	
		Flight Date	24.5.87		
Aeroplane Type	BLENHEIN MK IV	Pilot	J.F. LARCOMBE		
Registration	GMKIV	Observer	J. ROMAIN		
Aerodrome	DUXFORD	Aerodrome Alt.	120		ft.
Aerodrome Temp.	18 °C	QFE	1014		mb.

Weather Significant to Tests (e.g. Cloud base and tops, any turbulence)

4/8 Sc Base 2,500' Tops 4,000' SLIGHT CONVECTIVE TURBULENCE
SKS VIS BELOW 4000' UNLIMITED ABOVE

S 3/1/1

3. LOADING (For Details, see Appendix)

    > WARNING
    >
    > It is illegal to carry passengers on a test flight under "A" or "B" Conditions, except persons performing duties in the aircraft in connection with the flight.
    >
    > Airworthiness Flight Tests entail greater risk than normal flight, and although it may be legal to carry passengers on a test flight with a Certificate of Airworthiness in force, it is strongly recommended:-
    >
    > (a) that ballast should be used in order to comply with any prescribed loading requirements,
    >
    > (b) that the pilot in command should, before accepting any other persons on a test flight, inform them that the risk is greater than on an ordinary flight.

    Take-off Weight(actual)(kg/lb) | 11773 lb | c.g. Position (actual) | 12.9" AFT |

4. PRE-FLIGHT

    Flight Clearance authority issued and signed | YES |

    Check that the following items are on board:-

    (1) Aeroplane Flight Manual or other designated manual (e.g. Owner's Manual, Pilot's Operating Handbook, Pilot's Notes). | YES |

    (2) Cabin fire extinguisher (if applicable) | TWO B.C.F FITTED |

5. GROUND TESTS

    5.1 Equipment

        Check the following items for security and correct functioning:-

        | Fuselage and wing baggage compartment doors | SATISFACTORY |
        | Safety harness/lap straps | SATISFACTORY |
        | Door fastening | SATISFACTORY |
        | Adjustment of pilots' seats and locking. | SATISFACTORY |

    5.2 Controls

        Check for full travel, freedom and correct functioning:-

        Flying Controls

        | Elevator/Stabilator | FULL & FREE | Elevator/Stabilator trimmer | FULL RANGE. |
        | Ailerons | FULL & FREE | Rudder trimmer | FULL RANGE |
        | Rudder | FULL & FREE | Aileron trimmer | FIX TAB (GROUND ONLY) |
        | Wing-flaps | FULL RANGE & MOVEMENT | | |

        Engine Controls

	Left	Right
Throttle	FULL RANGE	FULL RANGE
Propeller pitch	TWO POSⁿ COARSE/FINE	TWO POSⁿ COARSE/FINE
Friction/locking mechanism	SATISFACTORY	SATISFACTORY
Mixture	NORMAL / WEAK	NORMAL WEAK
Carburettor heat	CORRECT INDICATIONS	CORRECT INDICATIONS
Alternate air intakes	N/A	N/A
Cooling flaps	COWLS FULL RANGE (E)	COWLS FULL RANGE (E)

        (E) - Electrically operated.

S3/1/2

5.3 Engine Run

	Left	Right
Ignition test RPM	2050 / 0" boost	2050 / 0" Boost
No.1 magneto off RPM drop	60	60
No.2 magneto off RPM drop	60	70
Carburettor hot air test RPM	1800 rpm	1800 r.p.m
Hot air RPM drop	70 rpm	80 rpm

Maximum Power Check

	Left	Right
Manifold pressure	0" Boost	0" Boost
RPM	2050	2050
Fuel pressure/flow (booster pump off)	2.5 psi	2.5 p.s.i
Fuel pressure/flow (booster pump on)	N/A	N/A

Right fuel pressure reads 5.5 psi – zero reading. 3.0 psi rise of 2.5 psi

NOTE: Care must be taken not to over-boost turbo-charged engines.
Do not exceed maximum permissible manifold pressure.

6. TAXYING

Brake system pressure	200 psi AIR PRESSURE
Parking brake (including Lock and Release)	NOT USED REQUIRES ADJUSTMENT.
Brakes(including freedom from binding and normal ability to hold aircraft at high engine power)	SATISFACTORY
Taxying (including nose-wheel steering/tail-wheel steering/ differential braking)	SATISFACTORY. ANTI-SHIMMY TAIL WHEEL TYRE FITTED, REAR OLEO AT 500psi CHARGE. MAKING SHARP TURNS WITHOUT DIFFERENTIAL POWER DIFFICULT.

7. TAKE-OFF

Wing-flap setting	0°	
Trimmer settings – Elevator/Stabilator	NEUTRAL – NEEDLE ON CENTRE/MARK	
– Rudder -Aileron	NEUTRAL	FIXED.
Behaviour during take-off:- Record any abnormal features, e.g. unusual tendency to swing, ease or difficulty of raising nose wheel/tail wheel, control forces (including any unusual control forces) or wing heaviness.	Nose is easily raised by elevator when full power applied for take-off. Very slight swing probably induced by differential power on acceleration, easily controlled by the powerful rudder.	
Was artificial stall warning triggered?	NOT FITTED	

S3/1/3

8.   CLIMB PERFORMANCE

Flight conditions: Not less than 3,000 feet above terrain, clear of cloud and
                   turbulence, and well clear of any hills which could produce
                   wave conditions.

Configuration: Normal for engine-out en-route climb (see Manual).

Power: Operative engine (see Appendix): Maximum Continuous with air
                  intake in "Cold" or "Ram" air position.
                  Inoperative engine: propeller feathered with cooling flap closed.

Altimeter: 1013 mb.(29.92 in.Hg.)

Speed: En-route climb speed(knots/mph.IAS)(See Appendix) | 105 mph |
        coarsen
Time to feather left/right propeller | 12   secs. |

Fuel Contents | 260 gals | Wing-flap position | 0° |
Weight (kg/lb) | 1870 lbs | Engine cooling -
at start of climb   flap position | CLOSED GILLS |

Time (min)	Altitude (ft) (1013 mb.)	IAS (knots/mph)	OAT (°C)
0	3000	105	+8°C
½	3300	105	
1	3450	102	+8°C
1½	3500	105	
2	3600	100	+5°C
2½	3600	105	
3	3700	105	+8°C
3½			
4			
4½			
5			

NOTE: If no Outside Air Temperature gauge is fitted, obtain the temperature at
the climb altitude for the local area from the Meteorological Office. State
whether the figure quoted is forecast (F) or indicated (I).

Towards the end of the climb record:-
Engine | Left/Right |
Manifold pressure* | 2.5 psi |
RPM | 2350 | Fuel pressure/flow | 2.5 psi |
Oil pressure | 70 psi | Cylinder head temperature | 175°C |
Oil temperature | 90°C |

Trimmer positions:-
Elevator/stabilator | NEUTRAL | Rudder | FULL LEFT. | Aileron | NIL |

If there is any difficulty in recording these figures during the timed climb,
maintain the climb speed and power, and record them at the end of the climb.

Restart engine and record:-

Unfeathering behaviour, including any | STARBOARD ENGINE IN COARSE PITCH TO
excessive vibration or roughness | SIMULATE DEAD ENGINE FINE |

   *Turbo-charged engines with automatic pressure controllers should maintain
        maximum permissible manifold pressure with the throttles fully forward.
   If the throttle cannot be opened fully without over-boosting, note throttle
   position at which maximum permissible manifold pressure is achieved (This will
   assist post flight rectification of the defect).

S3/1/4

9. STALLS

To be performed clear of cloud, with propeller controls fully fine and throttles closed. Recommended starting altitude for each stall not below 5000 feet above terrain.

Stall	1	2*	3
Landing Gear (unless fixed)	Up	Up	Down
Wing-flaps	Up	Take-off 15°	Landing
Trim, power off, at 1.5 x Scheduled stall speed (knots/mph IAS) ≠	105 mph.	100 mph	90 mph
Stall warning (knots/mph IAS)	SLIGHT BUFFET 77 mph.	SLIGHT BUFFET 75 mph	SLIGHT BUFFET 70 mph
Type of stall warning	NOSE NODS	NOSE GENTLY FALLS	NOSE GENTLY FALLS
Stall speed (knots/mph IAS)	74 mph	70 mph	60 mph
Scheduled stall speed (knots/mph IAS) ≠	70 mph	66 mph.	60 mph
Did control column reach back stop?	YES	NOT QUITE	YES
Sequence of nose and wing drop (if any)	N/A	N/A	SLIGHT LEFT WING DROP — 10°
Angle of wing drop	NIL	SLIGHT LEFT	10° MAX
Other characteristics	DOCILE	DOCILE	VERY GENTLE

* To be made on aeroplanes where a take-off wing-flap setting is specified.

≠ See Appendix.

10. FUNCTIONING TESTS - PART 1

Engine Control at Altitude (Turbo-charged engines only)

Climb to 10,000 feet at the scheduled en-route climb speed (2 engines) with the engine cooling flaps set as recommended (see Manual) and with propeller pitch controls fully forward. On engines with automatic pressure controllers, check that, with throttles fully forward, the manifold pressure does not exceed the maximum permissible, and can be maintained on each engine within 1 in.Hg. of the maximum permissible . Note any fluctuation of engine RPM, manifold pressure, or fuel flow/pressure and any tendency for the engine to overheat.

NOTES (1) At 10,000 feet on engines without automatic pressure controllers it will not usually be possible to set throttles fully forward without exceeding maximum permissible manifold pressure.

(2) If fuel pressure/flow fluctuates, switch on booster pump(s), reset fuel pressure/flow if necessary and note if indication is then steady.

Towards end of climb, record:-

Engine	Left	Right
Manifold pressure		
RPM		
Booster pump on/off		
Stability of RPM, Manifold pressure or fuel flow/ pressure		
Oil temperature		
Cylinder head temperature		

11. DIVE TO V_{NE} THIS TEST MUST ONLY BE DONE IN SMOOTH AIR CONDITIONS

Landing gear and wing-flaps retracted.
Accelerate the aeroplane in level flight using maximum continuous power, but with
propeller controls set to give approximately 200 RPM below maximum permissible.

Used 2½ lbs /2400 Throttled back to 2200 rpm / COARSE PITCH

In level flight, record:-

IAS (knots/mph)	215 mph	Elevator/Stabilator trimmer setting	SLIGHT NOSE DOWN
RPM left engine	2400	Rudder trimmer setting	NEUTRAL
right engine	2400	Aileron trimmer setting	N/A

Increase speed in a shallow dive up to V_{NE}. Keep RPM within maximum permissible.
If any unusual airframe or control vibration is felt, immediately reduce speed by
gradually pulling the control column back and by closing the throttles. Record:-

Any unusual behaviour	NO		
Whether the control forces and responses over small angles are normal	YES		
Steadiness of propeller governing (if applicable)	SLIGHT STEADY INCREASE WITH SPEED		
Maximum RPM	Left 2400	Right	2400
Maximum IAS (knots/mph)	260 mph		

Regain cruising flight by closing throttles and gradually pulling the control
column back.   Record:-

	Left	Right
Engine behaviour on closing throttles	NORMAL	NORMAL
Propeller governing (if applicable)	NORMAL	NORMAL

12. FUNCTIONING TESTS - PART 2

Check the following:-

12.1 Flying Controls

	Friction	Backlash	Are control forces normal?
Elevator/Stabilator	15lbs static	NIL	YES
Aileron	5lbs static	NIL	YES
Rudder	25lbs static	NIL	YES
Elevator/Stabilator Trimmer	N/A	NIL	YES
Rudder Trimmer	N/A	NIL	YES
Aileron Trimmer	N/A	N/A	N/A

During normal cruise, check that the aeroplane:-

(a) can be trimmed in pitch to fly level   YES

(b) has no tendency to fly one wing low   NO

(c) flies straight with slip indicator central   YES

S3/1/6

12.2 Engines

12.2.1 Check for excessive mal-alignment of throttles, pitch and mixture controls, when set to same power on each engine

> ALLIGNED

12.2.2 At a typical two engines en-route climb speed, shut down and re-start opposite engine to that shut down during engine-out climb. Record:-

Engine	BOTH ENGINES TESTED.
Time to feather (sec)	12 secs to COARSE, 6 secs to fine
Propeller unfeathering behaviour, including excessive vibration or roughness	FINE/COARSE/FINE NONE

12.3 Wing Flaps

Operate as follows, time operation and record any unusual change of longitudinal trim with flap position, and any significant change in lateral trim.

12.3.1 Flap selection
Operating time (sec)
Trim changes

From Up to Take-off*	From Take-off to Down*
3 secs	4 secs
NOSE DOWN	MORE NOSE DOWN

* At limiting speed for flap setting.   120 mph

12.3.2 Flap selection
Operating time (sec)
Trim changes

Down to Take-off ≠	Take-off to Up ≠
3 secs	2 secs.
NOSE UP	MORE NOSE UP

≠ At any convenient speed below limiting speeds.

12.4 Landing Gear-Normal Operation

Power-operated systems - time extension and retraction at limiting speed(s).

From Up to Down (sec)	From Down to Up (sec)
20 sees	22 sees.

Check landing gear unsafe warning. At a typical circuit speed with landing gear retracted, for each engine in turn select pitch control fully fine, and close throttle until warning sounds, record:-

Engine	Left	Right
Manifold Pressure	0.5	0 S
RPM	1000	1000

12.5 Fuel System

During the flight, feed each engine from each fuel tank in turn for not less than 3 minutes (normal and cross-feed).

Record:-

Engine	Left	Right
Left wing tank 1	CROSS FEED WORKS	BOTH WAYS FEEDING
Left wing tank 2	PORT TO STARBOARD AND VICE VERSA	
Right wing tank 1		
Right wing tank 2		
Auxiliary tank 1		
Auxiliary tank 2		
Fuel selector operation	CORRECT	
Fuel gauges	SATIS READING	SATIS. READING

12.6 Auto-pilot (if fitted)

Check for smooth engagement and disengagement, and general functioning during level flight, turn, climb and dive

N/A

With the auto-pilot engaged, apply a load to each main flying control and check satisfactory ability to overpower auto-pilot.

N/A

12.7 Electrical System

Check all electrical equipment for satisfactory operation, including load transfer switching left to right and right to left.

Only one generator fitted on PORT ENGINE.

Record ammeter readings with both generators on line

Left	Right
4-8 amp charge	at 2000 rpm.

Has ½ charge + full charge position operated from wireless op/air gunner position.

12.8 Flight Control Instruments

Check behaviour of instruments:-

Vacuum pump on PORT ENGINE

If air-pump driven, record: Press.gauge	− 3³/₄ psi	during cruise at	2000	RPM

12.9 Other Instruments

Check for satisfactory functioning:-

All instrumentation works satisfactorily.

12.10 De-Icing Equipment (if fitted).

Check functioning of systems for de-icing of:-

Airframe	N/A	Propeller	N/A	Windscreen	N/A

12.11 Radio

Complete attached Radio Flight Test Report.

12.12 Emergency Extension of Landing Gear

Extend the gear on the emergency system (only if the system is such that it can subsequently be reverted to normal operation in flight). Record operation:

> Not to be tested in the air. Tested frequently in the ground test schedule. Blow down system using CO_2 bottles using same piping via shuttle valves.

13. LANDING

With landing gear extended and wing-flaps in the landing position, carry out a normal landing following an approach at the speed specified in the Manual.

Behaviour during landing:
Record any abnormal features, e.g. unusual inability to trim, unusual control forces, difficulty in flaring, "wheelbarrowing" or porpoising after touch-down.

> Landed very easily, no difficulty encountered during landing roll.

Was artificial stall warning triggered?

> N/A

14. POST-FLIGHT

14.1 Placards

Check that all Cockpit, Cabin, Baggage Space and external placards are fitted and legible.

> all fitted and legible

14.2 Lighting

Check that all external and internal lighting is serviceable.

> Nav lights + landing lights sl. Internal lights serviceable.

14.3 Climb Performance

The observed figures for the climb are to be plotted on the attached graph and compared with the scheduled performance (see Appendix). It is important that the results are presented as observed, and that any significant meteorological conditions are noted.

NOTE: Where no correction for temperature is given in the designated Manual, the following temperature correction is to be applied:-

When the indicated outside air temperature is above International Standard Atmosphere for the altitude, the scheduled rate of climb may be reduced by 4 ft/min/°C (2.2 ft/min/°F). When the indicated OAT is below ISA, the scheduled rate of climb is to be increased by the same amount.

S3/1/9

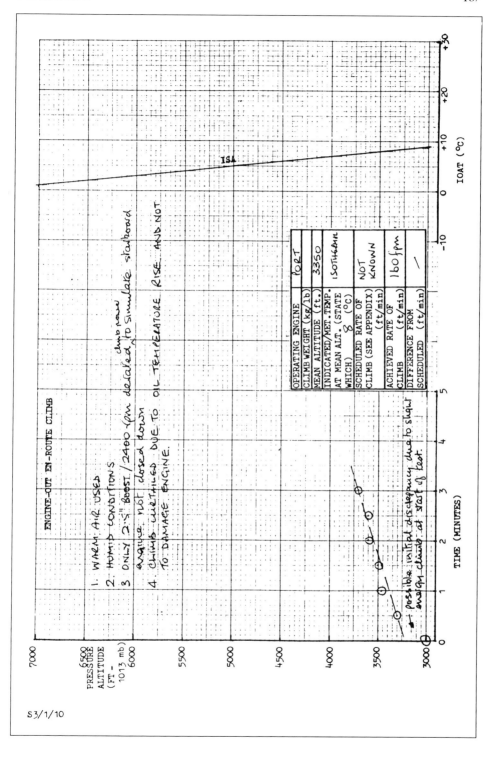

ENGINE-OUT EN-ROUTE CLIMB

1. WARM AIR USED
2. HUMID CONDITIONS
3. ONLY 2·5" BOOST/2400 fpm derated to simulate starboard engine not closed down
4. CLIMB CURTAILED DUE TO OIL TEMPERATURE RISE AND NOT TO DAMAGE ENGINE.

OPERATING ENGINE	PORT
CLIMB WEIGHT (kg/lb)	3350
MEAN ALTITUDE (ft.)	ISOTHERMAL
INDICATED/MET.TEMP. AT MEAN ALT. (STATE WHICH) δ (°C)	8
SCHEDULED RATE OF CLIMB (SEE APPENDIX) (ft/min)	NOT KNOWN
ACHIEVED RATE OF CLIMB (ft/min)	160 fpm
DIFFERENCE FROM SCHEDULED (ft/min)	/

ISA

IOAT (°C)

PRESSURE ALTITUDE (FT - 1013 mb)

7000
6500
6000
5500
5000
4500
4000
3500
3000

TIME (MINUTES)

← possible initial discrepancy due to slight shallow climb at start of test.

S3/1/10

FLIGHT TEST CERTIFICATE

I certify that I have carried out all the tests specified in Airworthiness
Flight Test Schedule No.3, Issue 1 and that the aeroplane was satisfactory
subject to rectification of the following.

DEFECTS AND UNDESIRABLE CHARACTERISTICS

Those annotated need a reflight.

	REFLIGHT NEEDED
I do not consider a reflight required on any major item. Only minor defects recorded which will be rectified and tested at a subsequent date.	NO

Flight Defects transcribed to ......F.700................. for rectification and
clearance.

Pilot ...John Larcombe.........   Licence Cat. and No. ..ATPL 94321....

Date ...24.5.87.......   Signed ...John Larcombe..........

S3/1/11

AIRWORTHINESS FLIGHT TEST SCHEDULE NO. 3,   ISSUE 1.
RADIO FLIGHT TEST REPORT

Aeroplane Type: ___BLENHEIM IV___   Part of Flight Test Report No.: ___1___

Registration: ___G.MKIV___   Date of test: ___24.5.87___

                     Pilot: ___JOHN LARCOMBE___

COMMUNICATIONS RADIO

Equipment	Type	Authorised* Ground Station	Freq.	A/C Position and Distance from Station†	Alt.†	Time (Z)	Reported Signal TX	Reported Signal RX
VHF COMM(1)		STANSTED LUTON	125.55 129.55	NORTH –10 mls EAST 30 mls	1000'–4500' 2000'	170-1800 1800	5/5	5/5
VHF COMM(2)								
HF COMM								

*See UK 'Air Pilot' or 'General Aviation Flight Guide' or contact CAA local Area Office.
† To be acceptable, a VHF Communication test must establish a minimum range of 20 nm from a height of 2000 ft above the ground station. At greater heights the range so established must be correspondingly greater.

NAVIGATION AIDS

	Type	Ground Station	Freq.	Aeroplane Position	Actual Radial	Audio Ident.	Flag Ind. of reliable signal?	Pointer Indication
VOR(1)		BARKWAY	113.4	O'HEAD DUXFORD	020°	YES	yes/no	Radial° 020 from/to
VOR(2)							yes/no	Radial° from/to
LOC(1)							yes/no	satis/unsatis
LOC(2)							yes/no	satis/unsatis
G/S(1)							yes/no	satis/unsatis
G/S(2)							yes/no	satis/unsatis

	Type	Beacon	Ground Station	Audio	Light
MARKER (LO setting if fitted)	N/A	Outer		satis/unsatis	satis/unsatis
		Middle		satis/unsatis	satis/unsatis

	Type	Ground Station	Freq.	Aeroplane Position	Heading	Actual Relative Bearing	Indicated Bearing
ADF(1)							
ADF(2)							

	Type	Ground Station	Freq.	Aeroplane Position	Range Actual	Range Indicated
DME						

	Type	Position Actual	Position Indicated	Error
AREA NAV				

MISCELLANEOUS

TRANSPONDER	Type	Ground Station	Code	Range	Alt.	Reported Signal
		LUTON LONDON	~~7225~~ 7230	50nms	3000'	RECEIVED BY LONDON

ENCODING ALTIMETER	Type	Indicated Altitude (1013 mb)	Reported Altitude
	N/A		

INTER-COMM	Type	Operation
	EXCELLENT — 5 position	WHEEL WELLS, NOSE, GUNNER, NAV + PILOT POSITIONS.

RADIO FLIGHT TEST DEFECTS

1. Radio worked well on all frequencies used.
2. Transponder received by London at 3000' in the Duxford area — range 50 nms.
3. VOR checked on various aircraft headings - switching the set on and off — signal received on correct radial each time.
4. Intercom - used in all positions except navigator, was excellent.

I consider the radios + intercom to be excellent, clear, and always audible. There is interference when using the electric gill motors which will be rectified.

I certify that the radio station designated overleaf has, in every respect, been found to perform satisfactorily in flight, with the exception of the items listed above, which have been transcribed to _____ for rectification and clearance.

Pilot _____ JOHN LARCOMBE _____

Signature _____ John Larcombe _____   Radio Licence No. ___ ATPL 94321. ___

S3/1/14

Re-airtest on Blenheim G-MKIV.

The following is the report on an airtest carried out to Blenheim G-MKIV, by Capt J.F. Larcombe, pilot, and J. Romain, observer.

The report should be read in conjunction with 'special' type airtest schedule, as applicable to vintage aircraft, which was supplied by the flight test dept, Redhill.

Blenheim G-MKIV

Airtest for issue of permit to fly   Dated 24.5.87

The aircraft handled extremely well on the first relatively short flight, on 22.5.87. The flying controls felt as expected, fairly heavy, especially when maintaining height in a turn. However, all air loads could be trimmed out with the use of the trimmers. Only minor system malfunctions occurred, which were to be expected (eg A/H not working correctly. A leak was found in the instrument, which was replaced, vacuum pressure restored and thereafter all instruments worked satisfactorily).

For both take-offs prior to the formal airtest and on the airtest itself I used 2½–3 lbs boost (4¼ rated), 2300 rpm, and climbed at 130 mph. The aircraft reached 3000' in 2 min 50 secs from start of take-off run. Quite an impressive rate of climb for a 50-year-old aircraft, using de-rated power.

The weather for the airtest was not ideal, 4/8 Cu base of 2500', tops 4000' humid between the clouds, slight turbulence, and a ground temp of 18°C. Because of the humidity I used carb heat.

Tests

2.1 Old pilot's notes with irrelevant details deleted.
2.2 Aircraft has been recently weighed. Basic weight of 9431 lbs. Take-off weight for the test was 11773 lbs with a C of Gravity position of 12.9 ins aft. The C of G range is 0 to 17.37 ins aft.
2.3 Knowledge has been obtained from a variety of sources, RAF Hendon, BAC and Bristol-Filton.
2.4 Signed by CAA surveyor and engineer in charge.
2.5 Issued.

Loading

3.a No ballast carried.
 b Observer informed of relevant risks.
3.1 Calculated and recorded.
3.2 Recorded. Aerobatics not to be flown.
3.3 Parachutes carried.

Cockpit and run up

4.1 All flying controls, trims and engine controls functioned correctly.

Mixture controls, Normal (rich) to the rear and down, Weak forward and up.

New harnesses and release mechanisms fitted, work extremely well.

The aircraft has been reglazed and the vision is excellent with proviso of the view whilst taxiing to the starboard of the nose. This is due to the aircraft's design. Both wing-tips can be seen.

4.2 The engines take a while to warm up due to the large oil tank capacity (loss of 12–16 pints/hour is normal, loss on the test flight, duration 1 hour 35 mins, was ½ pint stb'd and 3 pints port; the port engine was used for the single engine climb.)

   a The propellors both went from Fine-Coarse-Fine satisfactory.
   b Carb heat worked correctly with drop in rpm.
   c Oil cooler air shut-off worked correctly enabling a more rapid warm up of the oil.
   d Mixture controls satisfactory, rpm drop in weak.
   e Throttle friction functions well.
   f Engines run up to 0 lbs boost both giving 2050 rpm, ignition checks giving an rpm drop of 60, 60, 60, 70.

4.3 *Radio* was checked with Duxford 123.50, Stansted 125.55 and radar, and Luton 129.55, 2000' at 26 miles, all 5 by 5.

   VOR Checked on Barkway 113.40 — correct radial indicated and lock-ons occurred on a variety of headings and therefore various aerial positions presented to the beacon.

   Transponder Received by London at a height of 3000' in the Duxford area, coding as requested.

   Intercom Good reception in all tested positions, navigator, gunner and wheel bays.

   Compass DI works exceptionally well, very little drift over the 90 mins period.

   The main compass requires swinging, the E.2 stand-by compass works correctly.

Take-off

5.1 All trims set to neutral, trim indicators require adjustment so that full range of trim movement coincides with full design travel. At the moment full trim range is only indicated by ⅓ scale movement. However, it is considered to be adequate. The elevator and rudder have variable trims, the ailerons a fixed tab which can be set on the ground only, if required.

5.2 At weights below 14000 lbs (12500 lbs is the max to be used on G-MKIV) 0° flap is to be used for take off.

5.3 I had the take-off run measured to give a rough guide as to T/O performance. Wind conditions 050/12 (headwind 12 kts). The ground run was 500 m.

5.4 Tailwheel can be raised immediately T/O power is applied. However, on the airtest take-off I attempted to accelerate tail down and left the ground at about 75–80 mph. Very little swing occurred on any take-off and as such was easily controlled by the effective rudder.

5.5   Accelerated to 130 mph, nose down trim required as expected.

5.6   No stall warning fitted, no stall warning occurred.

Asymmetric handling Vmca

6.1   No difference between engines detected. Power used 3 lb boost at 2400 rpm, Vmca 82–85 mph. Largest bank angle achieved was

6.2   30° to starboard, corrected with full rudder, and using 5′ bank into the live engine. If speed is reduced to less than

6.3   82 mph the engine-induced yaw is uncontrollable. Full rudder takes quite a leg force to apply and maintain. However, as speed increases less rudder is required, which is to be expected.

6.4   We cannot feather either engine; propellers can be in fine or coarse. Fine to coarse takes 12 secs, coarse to fine takes 6 secs. On each engine is a fuel-lubricated fuel pump, and the only way to totally close down an engine is to shut off the fuel. However, the engine would keep turning and probably lead to a break-down of the pump. I therefore considered it unwise to actually shut an engine down.

Climb

7   I only climbed for 3 minutes, as the oil temp rose to the limit on the powered engine, and the oil press commenced to fall. We used 2½ lbs boost at 2350–2400 rpm in fine pitch, climbing at 130 mph. Carb heat was selected due to the humid conditions. The climb was difficult to fly due to atmospheric conditions and was very speed critical. However, with all the conditions against the aircraft, ie Carb heat, derated power at 2½ instead of 4¼ lbs boost, and slight turbulence, it climbed quite well, 700′ in 3 mins. The engine used also carries all the ancillaries (generator, hydraulic pump, vacuum pump) so was assessed to be the most critical as to power output.

Stick force per 'G'

8   210 mph with 60 degree bank. 30 lb pull required to maintain the speed and turn. Turning requires quite a pull as mentioned in the pilot's notes.

Stalls

9.1   Clean — 74 mph, gentle nodding, stick fully back. 15 flap — 70 mph, gentle nodding, stick nearly full back. Full flap, u/c down — 60 mph, slight wing drop, slight buffet, stick fully back.
      All stalls were very gentle with no unexpected characteristics.

9.2   Power 1½ boost, 1800 rpm, 66 mph — no stall, very high nose attitude, stick nearly on back stops.

9.3   30° bank to left, buffet at 78 mph, 74 mph slightly more buffet, very gentle.
      30° bank to right, more and more opposite aileron required to maintain 30° bank. I considered it unwise to reduce speed lower than 80 mph. We

had at that time a 30 gal (220 lb) assymetric fuel load on the right side.

Rates of roll
10.1 MCP gear and flaps down, 4 secs to roll 60°, 30° right to 30° left.
10.2 MCP gear and flaps up, 5 secs to roll 60°, 30° right to 30° left.
10.3 200 mph, clean, 2–3 secs to roll 60°, 30° right to 30° left.

Change of trim with speed and power
11.1 Nose down trim required, approx ¾ turn. Max speed 215 mph, speed
      increased to 260 mph. All control forces normal and linear. No buzz or
      flutter found. Obviously the aircraft feels heavier and control forces
      increase markedly. Engine rpms increase with speed and you have to
      throttle back to make sure the rpm limits are not exceeded. When
      throttled back, engine behaviour was normal.

Change of stick force with power
12.1 Nose up trim change, 10 lb push required to maintain speed.
12.2 Nose up trim change, 12 lb push required to maintain speed.

Change of stick force with flap
13.1 Nose down, 12 lb pull.
13.1 Nose down, 17 lb pull.
13.3 Nose up, 20 lb push.

Baulk landing
14.1 Aircraft climbs easily, large nose up trim change which can be controlled
      with control column. 20 lb push required to maintain IAS.

Lateral and directional stability
15.1 Satisfactory.
15.2 The aircraft has a +ve lateral stability.
15.3 The aircraft has a +ve directional stability.
      No unusual characteristics found.

Longitudinal stability
16.1 15 lb push, nose rotates upwards. Decreasing speed, 8 lb pull, nose falls.
16.2 No trim change, slight nose rise. Very little trim change, slight fall.

Controllability sideslips
      Not required.

Minimum trim speeds
18.1-18.5 Aircraft can be trimmed load free in all cases.

Auto-pilot
19.0 Not fitted.

Functioning checks

20.1 (1) Friction, measured before flight: Ailersons 5 lbs
                                                Elevators 15 lbs
                                                Rudder 25 lbs
       (2) No backlash.
       (3) In flight heavy but all normal.
       (4) No unusual characteristics.

20.2 (1) Yes
       (2) No
       (3) Yes

20.3 (1) 12 secs at 1500 rpm.   Hyd pressure is a direct
       (2)   5 secs at 1500 rpm.   function of engine rpm. Full flap is also slow
                          to deploy at max IAS 120 mph.

20.4 (1) 20 secs U/c cycles port first, then starboard,
       (2) 22 secs due to the hydraulic pump being on the port engine. There
                      is a slight asymmetric effect due to the starboard leg lagging
                      behind the port, but nothing significant.

20.5 Crossfeed works.

20.6 Generator on port engine, controlled by rear crew member. ½ or full
      charge dependent on battery condition. 8 amps charge normal.

20.7 Vacuum pump, on port engine. 3¾ at 2000 rpm. All instruments work
      well.

20.8 All satisfactory.

20.9 All radio stations used 5/5. VOR satisfactory, intercom excellent.
      Transponder received 50 nms at 3000' by London.

20.10 By agreement, not tested in flight. Tested on ground frequently. The
      system uses blow-down CO_2 bottles via shuttle valves which blow the
      legs down; the CO_2 also contaminates the hyd system once used.

20.11 Handling behaviour excellent, no tendency to swing. A 'g' meter is
      fitted in the bomb bay to monitor A/C fatigue and any exedences. I
      suggest 2½ 'G' – 70° bank level turn.

Signed: J.J. Romain   pp J.F. Larcombe   ATPL 94321

CAA Permit to Fly and Exemption

United Kingdom
Civil Aviation Authority

Permit to Fly

No. ......PR-1251-1......

Nationality and Registration Marks	Constructor and Constructor's Designation of Aircraft	Aircraft Serial No. (Constructor's No.)
G-MKIV	Fairchild Bolingbrooke MK 4T	10038

Classification: Ex Military Aircraft

Purposes for which the aircraft may fly: Demonstration and Exhibition

Documents associated with this Permit: Pilots Notes A.P. 1530B/G-MKIV

Operator of the aircraft: British Aerial Museum

Engine type: Bristol Mercury XX

Propeller type: DH Type 4/3

Maximum number of occupants authorised to be carried (including crew):   Three

The Civil Aviation Authority in exercise of its powers under the Air Navigation Order, hereby permits the aircraft specified above to fly within the United Kingdom only, without a Certificate of Airworthiness being in force in respect thereof.

This Permit is issued subject to the Conditions shown overleaf.

Date   29th May 1987

for the Civil Aviation Authority

This Permit is valid for the period(s) shown below		Official Stamp and Date
From 29th May 1987	to 28th May 1988	C.A.A.
From	to	
From	to	
From	to	
From	to	

NOTE: This permission for flight within the United Kingdom is not a Certificate of Airworthiness issued pursuant to the Convention on International Civil Aviation dated 7th December 1944.

No entries or endorsements may be made on this Permit except by an authorised person. If this Permit is lost, the Civil Aviation Authority should be informed at once. Any person finding this Permit should forward it immediately to the Civil Aviation Authority, Airworthiness Division, Brabazon House, Redhill, Surrey RH1 1SQ.

CA 960B
071186

CONDITIONS OF THE PERMIT

1   The aircraft shall be operated only by the operator named on Page 1.

2   The aircraft shall not be flown for the purpose of public transport or aerial work.

3   The aircraft shall not be flown over any assembly of persons or over any congested area of a city, town or settlement.

4   The aircraft shall not be flown unless the pilot in command has satisfied himself that it is in an adequate state of repair and in sound working order.

5   The aircraft shall be operated in accordance with the procedures and limitations contained in the appropriate technical publications and manufacturers instructions and recommendations for the type and model of aircraft, or in compliance with the limitations specified in the Documents associated with this Permit.

6   No alterations, modifications or replacements shall be made to this aircraft or to its engines, propellers, or equipment, unless approved by the CAA or other Organisations approved by the CAA for the purpose.

7   A permanent placard shall be affixed to the aircraft in full view of the occupants, and shall be worded as follows:

OCCUPANT WARNING
THIS AIRCRAFT HAS NOT BEEN CERTIFICATED TO AN INTERNATIONAL REQUIREMENT

8   A Certificate that the aircraft has been inspected and is fit for flight shall be in force during all flights. The operator shall not permit the aircraft to fly unless this certificate has been issued within the preceding five hours flying time or seven days, whichever is the lesser. This certificate shall only be issued by such persons as are authorised by the CAA.

9   Notwithstanding any exemption from registration or from the bearing of registration marks, this aircraft shall comply with all other requirements of the Air Navigation Order as if it were registered in the United Kingdom.

10   The aircraft shall not be flown for the purpose of public transport or aerial work, except aerial work which consists of flights for the purpose of public exhibition or demonstration, including practice flights, test flights and positioning flights associated with such demonstration.

11   The minimum flight crew is: One   pilot   but see Condition 13

12   The aircraft must be operated in compliance with the following operating limitations, which shall be displayed in the crew compartment by means of placards or instrument markings:

12.1 **Aerobatic limitations:**
     Intentional spinning is prohibited. Aerobatic manoeuvres are prohibited.

12.2 **Loading limitations:**   SEE PILOTS NOTES
     Maximum Total Weight Authorised:
     C.G. range limits   inches to   inches aft of the datum point which is the leading edge of the
     wing.

12.3 **Engine limitations:**
     Maximum engine RPM: SEE PILOTS NOTES
     Maximum engine RPM for continuous operation:

12.4 **Airspeed limitations:**
     Maximum indicated airspeed   mph (knots)   SEE PILOTS NOTES

12.5 **Other limitations:**
     The aircraft shall only be flown by day and under Visual Flight Rules.
     Smoking in the aircraft is prohibited.

13.   See attached sheet
CA 960B

United Kingdom
Civil Aviation Authority

Air Navigation Order

Exemption

No. ER-1251-1

Nationality and Registration Marks	Constructor and Constructor's Designation of Aircraft	Aircraft Serial No. (Constructor's No.)
G-MKIV	Fairchild Bolingbrooke MK 4T	10038

Classification: Ex Military Aircraft

Purposes for which the aircraft may fly: Demonstration and Exhibition

Documents associated with this Exemption: Permit to Fly Number PR-1251-1

Operator of the aircraft: British Aerial Museum

The Civil Aviation Authority in exercise of its powers under the Air Navigation Order, hereby exempts the aircraft specified above from the provisions of the said Order to the extent that the said aircraft, when flying in accordance with the Permit to Fly and conditions thereof, is not restricted to making flights which begin and end in the United Kingdom and do not pass over any other country.

Date   29th May 1987   *for the Civil Aviation Authority*

This Exemption is valid for the period(s) shown below			Official Stamp and Date
From 29th May 1987	to	28th May 1988	**C.A.A.**
From	to		
From	to		
From	to		
From	to		

NOTE: This authorisation for flight within the United Kingdom is not a Certificate of Airworthiness issued pursuant to the Convention on International Civil Aviation dated 7th December 1944.

Permission for flight over any foreign country must be obtained from the airworthiness authority of that country.

No entries or endorsements may be made on this Exemption except by an authorised person. If this Exemption is lost the Civil Aviation Authority should be informed at once. Any person finding this Exemption should forward it immediately to the Civil Aviation Authority, Airworthiness Division, Brabazon House, Redhill, Surrey RH1 1SQ.

CA 961A
071186

Accident Investigation Board Report

Accident Investigation Board Report

No: 11/87   **Ref: 1a**

Aircraft type and registration:	Bristol 149 Blenheim Mk IV G-MKIV
No & Type of engines:	2 Bristol Mercury XX piston engines
Year of Manufacture:	1942
Date and time (UTC):	21 June 1987 at 1345 hrs
Location:	Denham airfield, Buckinghamshire
Type of flight:	Air display
Persons on board:	Crew — 3 Passengers — None
Injuries:	Crew — 3 (minor) Passengers — N/A
Nature of damage:	Aircraft damaged beyond repair
Commander's Licence:	Airline Transport Pilot's Licence
Commander's Age:	60 years
Commander's Total Flying Experience:	15,639 hours (of which $4\frac{1}{2}$ were on type)
Information Source:	Aircraft Accident Report Form submitted by the pilot, report by engineer and video film.

The aircraft was making an appearance at an air display. On board were the pilot and 2 engineers who were part of the team that had rebuilt the aircraft. One of the engineers, who knew the aircraft well and held a Private Pilot's Licence, Group B, occupied the right-hand cockpit seat for take-off and landing. The other engineer sat in the turret. The runway in use was 25 with a usable length of 667 metres; the wind was from the north-west at 3 to 5 knots and there was no significant weather.

When the display was planned the pilot had declined to land at Denham because of the relative shortness of the runway, and it had been agreed that no landing would be attempted. Nevertheless, on the day, after demonstrating the aircraft at both high and low speeds the pilot decided to carry out a touch-and-go landing. He later stated that he had been asked to do this by the display organisers but no evidence was found that any such request was made to him at the time of the display. The touch-and-go landing was thus not part of the planned display and had not been rehearsed.

A setting of 15° flap was used for the approach, which was shallower and slightly faster than it would have been if landing flap (60°) had been used. The aircraft touched down some way beyond the landing threshold and bounced slightly. The pilot controlled the bounce and applied power to take-off again. The sound of misfiring was heard from at least one engine and black smoke was seen behind the aircraft. The aircraft veered to the left and ran on to the grass. The pilot stated that after touch-down he steadily opened the throttles to +2 psi boost pressure then, sensing that the aircraft was not accelerating normally, he opened the throttle further. Acceleration was still below normal so he opened the throttles fully and then held th

1

aircraft on the ground to achieve flying speed. He had no recollection of the engines misfiring or of the aircraft swinging to the left. The engineer in the right-hand seat said that, after controlling the bounce, the pilot rapidly opened the throttles and both engines suffered rich mixture cuts. He said that he advised the pilot to close the throttles and open them up again more slowly but the pilot did not respond; some seconds later the right engine picked up to full power and the aircraft left the runway. The engineer in the turret confirmed that he heard on his headset the advice given by the other engineer to the pilot.

A video film of the landing showed the aircraft rolling along the runway with the tailwheel off the ground for about 12 seconds, for the last 8 of which the sound of an engine or engines misfiring could be heard on the film. The right wing then began to rise and the aircraft ran off the runway with the right wing still rising, at a speed said by the pilot to have been about 80 mph but thought by the engineer to have been about 70 mph. It became airborne, banked some 15° to the left, and climbed to between 50 and 100 feet with the left bank increasing and the airspeed reducing. A few seconds later the left wing hit trees and the aircraft cartwheeled along the ground. Both engines were torn from their mountings, both wings were severely damaged and the fuselage was broken in half. The occupants suffered only minor injuries; the two engineers were able to evacuate the aircaft unaided and the pilot was released from the wreckage by the airport fire and rescue services, who arrived at the scene very quickly and covered leaking fuel with foam.

The operating company had taken great pains to ensure that the aircraft was airworthy and that the pilot was capable of safely performing the display. Prior to flying the Blenheim the pilot had been given experience on a Beechcraft 18, an aircraft with similar handling characteristics. He had flown 4½ hours on the Blenheim but had not practiced a touch and go landing on the aircraft. The Pilot's Notes stated that on take-off the throttles should be fully opened in a time of only 2 to 3 seconds and it had been found that any attempt to open the throttles in less than that time caused rich mixture cutting. The pilot was aware of the need to avoid rapid throttle movements.

Letter, G. Warner to R. Pullan, 6 August 1987

Dear Roy,

I am sorry that you have chosen not to speak to me since the accident as it is most important for all concerned that you fully understand the real, as opposed to any hypothetical, conjectural or imagined causes of it.

My first concern was the safety and return to health of all the crew so the enquiries as to the causes were left until recovery was assured.

Careful questioning of the surviving crew members who had a clear recollection of the accident, study of statements made by them to the A.I.B., Lloyd's and the C.A.A., and from various independent witnesses (including several ex-Blenheim pilots), plus close scrutiny of photographs and videos of the accident, and of the aircraft itself, lead to the inescapable conclusion from all concerned in the investigations that the entire responsibility for the accident was yours and yours alone.

You will find this conclusion difficult and painful to accept, but the truth is often so difficult and painful that it can be rejected as totally unacceptable by a mind seeking alternatives. The initial subconscious defence against such a traumatic shock as this accident is total or partial amnesia of events leading up to the shock itself. This is usually followed by periods of selective recall and attempts to rationalise the situation to make it more acceptable to the conscious mind; including convincing oneself that one took all the correct actions to prevent the accident, even if all the evidence demonstrates that this was not the case, as in this instance.

The correct sequence of events and the actual causes of the accident were as follows:

A/.   1) You took off from Duxford at 1355 hours local on Sunday 21st June with John Romain in the right-hand seat and John Smith in the rear position. There was slight oil smoke from both engines on starting and taxiing as is normal on radial piston-engines. Both engines were perfectly satisfactory on the run-up, on take-off and during the one low 'fly-by' you did some 8 minutes later before leaving for Denham. This is confirmed by the crew, our entire team, countless witnesses and many photographs and videos taken at the time. To suggest, as you are now doing, that a 'puff of smoke from the left-hand engine' at Duxford showed signs of some unknown engine trouble that manifested itself over 40 minutes later at Denham is completely fallacious.

2) On setting course for Denham at 1403 you asked John Romain to assist with the navigation, so he used the nav. position in the nose. The aircraft tracked via Barkway VOR, Ware and Brookmans Park VOR: you talked to ATC at both Hatfield and Leavesden en route and arrived in the Denham area at 1420 — the Concorde was just completing its demonstration. Denham ATC asked you to hold while three Turbulents displays and you were cleared in at 1432.

3) Before starting your Display John checked with you and confirmed that all engine temperatures and pressures were normal and that you had selected 'Normal' Mixture from the 'Weak' Mixture, used for the en route cruise; Carb Air 'Hot' and 'Course' Pitch was still selected at that stage. Four or five smooth passes linked by turns were flown down to about 200 feet with the aircraft in the 'clean' configuration; the aircraft performed perfectly throughout.

4) He then noticed you pumping the hydraulic hand-pump and called you on the intercom to ask about the problem — you replied that 'you wanted to do a "slow" flypast and had selected undercarriage "down" but it wasn't functioning'. He then rejoined you in the cockpit and found that the undercarriage selector was not fully in the 'down' position as the Carb Air controls were still in the 'Hot' position. He therefore selected 'Cold' Air and re-selected undercarriage 'down' and the system functioned correctly, but slower than on a normal downwind leg as in the usual downwind Vital Actions — Brakes 'off' Undercarriage 'Down' Mixture 'Rich' Pitch 'Fine' etc; the selection of 'Fine' Pitch raises the engine RPM and the output of the hydraulic pump and speeds the lowering of the undercarriage.

5) On the base leg for the 'slow' flypast John went through the pre-landing checks and found that the props were still in 'Course' Pitch, informed you of this and that he was selecting 'Fine'; you said 'Thankyou' and asked for 20° of Flap, which he set and confirmed to you.

6) You will recall that when you turn the hydraulic-power selector-control to the 'flaps and undercarriage' sector (prior to selecting either) it turns off the hydraulic power to the turret; so John Romain informed John Smith 'Power to turret off' — fortunately, although

not fore-and-aft, the guns were 'up' ie the seat was 'down' and Smith was able to vacate the turret — this certainly saved his life. The Captain should inform the occupant of the turret before moving the hydraulic-power selector-control and cutting off the power to the turret, so that the occupant can set it fore-and-aft, lower the seat and leave the turret; you had failed to do so.

7)   Therefore John Romain was carrying out his duties very ably and helping you materially. Up to that point, apart from nav assistance, and checking engine pressure and temps, he had:

a)   Reminded you to change from 'Weak' to 'Normal' Mixture.
b)   Selected Carb Air 'Cold'.
c)   Selected Undercarriage 'Down' properly.
d)   Selected Pitch 'Fine'.
e)   Informed Smith that the power to the turret was off.
f)   Completed the pre-landing checks.

— all vitally important items that you should have carried out yourself but didn't.

8)   The 'slow' flypast was carried out down the main runway at about 100 feet with the following settings:

a)   Undercarriage 'Down'.
b)   Mixture 'Normal'.
c)   Pitch 'Fine'.
d)   Carb Air 'Cold'.
e)   Flaps at 20 degrees.
f)   Sufficient power to maintain 100/105 mph IAS.

On completion of the 'slow' pass the aircraft climbed away very well although you told John to leave the undercarriage and flaps down. Denham ATC said 'Thank you for a very nice Display' — they thought you had completed your demonstration as your 'slot' was up. You replied 'Thank you very much, I'm coming in for a "touch-and-go" before departing'. Although surprised as it had not been pre-arranged, they gave the 'surface wind 2 to 4 knots, North Westerly'. John queried your decision to carry out this manoeuvre as he knew it would be marginal, saying 'Is this touch-and-go really necessary?' and you answered 'I am flying the aircraft, pre-landing checks please'. John ran through them again and confirmed that the aircraft was 'ready to land except that you had only 20° of flap'. (John Smith has confirmed these exact conversations from notes he made — without any reference to John Romain — on the evening of 21st June.)

9)   *Your decision to carry out the 'touch-and-go' manoeuvre was the fundamental cause of the accident* and was completely wrong because:

a)   You had not practised the manoeuvre in the Blenheim, although you had opportunity to do so at Duxford and Biggin Hill where the runways are longer and therefore safer, and away from the pressures of an Air Display.

b) You did not have sufficient time on the aircraft or familiarity with its systems to attempt such a manoeuvre.

c) You broke the 'Golden Rule' of Air Displays — 'Never attempt any manoeuvre without adequate rehearsal beforehand'.

d) You were aware that the length of runway 25 at Denham is only 667 m, that there was virtually no wind, and the ambient temperature was high.

e) Your own co-pilot and engineer, who knows the aircraft better than anyone, queried your decision as he was most apprehensive, but was over-ruled.

f) In all these circumstances sound airmanship would rule out any such attempt which, even if carried out successfully, would have hazarded the aircraft to an unacceptable degree.

g) The Chairman of the H.A.A. is quoted as saying that 'to attempt a touch-and-go in that aircraft at Denham is the most appalling example of bad airmanship at an Air Display that he had come across' — all of the expert pilots assembled there that day who have spoken to me, agreed.

h) You had agreed with both myself and the organisers beforehand *that no attempt at a landing at Denham would be made* and the organisers and the crew had been so informed. I, the crew, and the Team were all much relieved at this agreement and appalled that you should break it so blatantly.

10) You are incorrect to state in your letter that 'Denham ATC requested a touch-and-go' — they are quite clear that you informed them that you intended to carry out the manoeuvre and were surprised when you announced your intention. Both the other crew members confirms this sequence of events. It seems to have been a 'spur of the moment' decision resulting from the ATC praise of your display up to that point.

But if, as you now claim in your letter of the 29th June, 'you had planned the whole manoeuvre carefully in advance' this would have been a devious and grossly irresponsible deception of myself, the crew, and the organisers in view of the agreement that no attempt at a landing would be made. You now attempt to justify your actions and the ill-fated attempt by saying 'I gave some considerable thought to the manoeuvre .... I decided to eliminate any concept, or element, of a landing that was subsequently converted to a take off'. This can only be seen as an evasion of your clear agreement not to attempt a landing at Denham, for a 'touch-down and go-around again' nevertheless puts the aircraft on the ground prior to the overshoot and arguably entails greater risks than a full-stop landing.

11)   Similarly you state in the same letter that 'it is unfair of me (the owner) to leave such decisions to the Pilot' — but *only* the pilot can make that type of decision. You had been asked to look into the possibility of landing at Denham which the organisers would have preferred, but when you decided that it would be too risky we all instantly and happily accepted your decision and reached clear agreement not to attempt to land there. It would be quite wrong of me to impose on any Pilot such decisions as whether to land or not, to set out if the weather was marginal, to carry out a sortie if there was a problem with the aircraft, etc, and I have never done so. I have always left such operational decisions entirely to the discretion of the Pilot-in-Command, quite correctly, and have not attempted to influence them apart from insisting that 'the safety of the aircraft must be paramount' — not as you describe it 'as a rider' but as a fundamental requirement.

Any logical person can only treat these statements of yours as spurious post-event attempts to justify and rationalise the actions you took, and to evade responsibility for them.

B/.   The 'touch-and-go' manoeuvre itself was badly executed leading to a highly dangerous situation, compounded by your gross mis-handling of the engines and was turned into a disaster by your failure to take any corrective action whatsoever when it was clearly apparent that the aircraft, although still on the ground, was not accelerating sufficiently to climb away safely.

This is a statement of fact — not opinion, conjecture or surmise.

Careful analysis of all the evidence shows the actual sequence of events during this manoeuvre to be:

1)   The base leg was good at about 105 mph and the aircraft turned Finals and reduced speed to about 90; the aircraft lost height too rapidly over the small wooded valley on the approach and power was applied to reduce the rate of sink and correct the undershoot. Once the trees were passed all the power was pulled off but with the aircraft not in the correct landing attitude (ie with the tail too high with a low angle-of-attack, too shallow an approach, too high an airspeed and with the flap at a 'lift' not a 'drag' setting) it floated over half the length of the runway. A prudent pilot would have initiated an overshoot once it was apparent that the aircraft was not going to touch down near the threshold, but you allowed the aircraft to continue until it finally touched down far too deep into the available runway. You had 'boxed' the aircraft into a situation growing ever more dangerous by the second, rapidly running out of distance, height and time in which to retrieve the situation.

2)   The eventual touch down was hard and on one wheel first and, during the first bounce which you 'caught' by moving the control

column forward with your left hand to the neutral position, you attempted to apply full power by suddenly opening both throttles completely and very rapidly with your right hand. This action, probably instinctive but certainly not correctly executed, turned the already dangerous situation into which you had placed the aircraft and crew, into the disaster that followed.

3)   The inevitable result of this over-hasty application of power was a 'Rich Cut' on both engines as they attempted to meet this excessive demand — surges of power being followed almost instantly by loud 'bang backs' and engine cuts, with the cycle rapidly repeating, and the rev counters and boost gauges fluctuating wildly. The initial black rich-mixture smoke and all the sounds and symptoms of a 'rich cut' are clearly apparent on videos and photographs, and were witnessed and reported by many of the top pilots (including several ex-Blenheim pilots) who saw and heard it, as well as from the reliable testimony of the crew.

4)   John Romain called on the intercom. 'Pull them back — feed it in again' — there was no response. He called several times for you to 'pull them back' (this is substantiated by John Smith) and even tried physically to pull the throttles back, but your right hand was rigid and holding them fully open.

5)   The aircraft was still running along the runway at about 70 mph with the tail almost down throughout this period — some 8 or 9 seconds — and there was still sufficient room to abandon the attempt to 'go round again'. The correct action should have been to close the throttles, brake hard with the stick right back, turn off the magnetos, pull the engine cut-offs and (if there was time) turn off the fuel, and if the aircraft had still not slowed sufficiently, ground-loop it at the end of the runway. At the very worst it would have run into the hedge at about 10 mph.

6)   All your training and experience should have caused you to take these actions, *but you took no action at all*, despite John's ever more insistent calls. You sat, with your left-hand holding the control column neutral and your right-hand holding the throttles fully open, staring fixedly ahead, deaf to John's shouts, and unaware of his efforts to close the throttles.

7)   The starboard engine then picked up to full power for a few seconds and the aircraft left the runway to the left and ran across the grass for a further 3 to 4 seconds before becoming airborne again, still turning to the left, and about 100 yards from the airfield boundary. Timing the video shows the aircraft running along the ground for 12 to 13 seconds before flying again — ample time to attempt to stop it. The video also shows the rudder in the central position throughout so you did not even attempt to maintain directional control.

8)   The aircraft climbed to about 80 to 100 feet (estimates vary) and as the airspeed decayed through 65 to 60 John called 'You're going to

stall — look out, you're going to stall!' but still you took no action, and the port wing dropped. Just before the port wing-tip struck some trees on the Golf Course the port engine picked up too, and it might just have been possible to salvage the situation even at that late stage and climb away, if you had kept control of the aircraft and not just sat there.

9) The aircraft cartwheeled on to its nose and starboard wing-tip, both engines were torn right off, and the fuselage was broken in two at the turret. The position of the propeller blades shows that both engines were under power at the moment of impact, the port more so than the starboard. After the accident the controls were found in the following positions:

a) Undercarriage selected 'Down' (and locked down).
b) Flaps selected partially 'Down' — about 15 to 20 degrees.
c) Throttles — both fully open.
d) Mixture Controls — both 'Normal'.
e) Pitch Controls — both 'Fine'.
f) Carb Heat Controls — both on 'Cold Air'.
g) Carb Cut-offs — both in.
h) Magnetos — all 4 switches 'On'.
i) Fuel cocks — both 'On'.
j) Trimmers — Elevator slightly tail-heavy, Rudder neutral.

After the accident it was found that both engines turned fully and freely and each still had 9 compressions; there was no sign at all of any mechanical failure. The only possible conclusion is that both engines were running perfectly and capable of giving full power, as they did on the climb out from the 'slow fly-past' only a few minutes earlier, and that the lack of response to your mental demand for instant power was due solely to the physical mishandling of the controls resulting in a 'rich cut'.

10) When you finally 'touched' the runway John Romain was standing by for your command for 'full (or climbing) power' when he would have opened the throttles carefully and progressively, as he had practised overshoots in the Beech 18. This is normal practice in the services and BA when the right-hand seat is occupied by a qualified person. If you did not want to follow this established practice you should have fully briefed him on this beforehand.

   He was shocked when you slammed them wide open yourself, but despite his efforts he was unable to correct your mistake, the results of which he could see, feel, and hear.

11) You had been fully briefed on the necessity to open the throttles slowly, smoothly and progressively (especially in undershooting or 'going round again' situations), by myself, John Larcombe and John Romain. You were well aware that Pilot's Notes gives three full seconds as the optimum time for opening the throttles and yet you

took about half-a-second.

You knew that Mercury engines have updraught carburettors with very powerful accelerator pumps, and that the supercharger is clutch-driven from the crankshaft and takes several seconds to 'spin up' and deliver the correct fuel/air ratio for an accelerating engine. You claim now to have 'opened them up carefully' and then to have 'opened them up some more when they didn't respond, up to +2 lbs boost' yet both the RPM and Boost Gauges were fluctuating widely as the engines cut, picked up, coughed, and cut again in the classic 'rich cut'. This selective 'recall' is from your subconscious mind which knows *what you should have done*, probably what you *meant* to do, in trying to convince your conscious mind that this is what you actually did and that there must be some other explanation for the lack of power.

All the evidence points to the inescapable conclusion that there is no other possible explanation apart from a 'rich cut' on both engines caused solely by opening the throttles in the heat of the moment far too quickly.

Incidentally, a spokesman from Denham told the media that 'an engine had failed so that the aircraft was unable to climb away after a touch-and-go and crash landed on the Golf Course'. That was the origin of that rumour. I refrained from any comment as to the cause until all the facts were known.

C/.   So it has been demonstrated beyond doubt that the entire responsibility for destroying this unique aircraft, which was an important and priceless part of our aviation heritage, rests fairly and squarely on you alone, as:

1)   Your decision to attempt a 'touch and go' at Denham was a most serious mis-judgement whether premeditated or spontaneous.
2)   The manoeuvre itself was badly executed leading to a most dangerous situation.
3)   This situation was turned into a potentially fatal disaster by gross mis-handling of the engine controls.
4)   When faced with the result of this series of mis-judgements and errors you failed totally to take any of the normal actions to abandon the overshoot and retrieve the situation by stopping the aircraft while it was still on the ground.
5)   That the crew escaped with their lives is a pure miracle considering the severity of the accident and that you had not been in effective control of the aircraft at all once it had touched down.

D/.   For you to write in your letter of the 29th June that John Romain 'had vacated the cockpit not to re-appear' and that 'this was not the sort of co-operation that I expect from a crew member' and apportioning part of the blame to him, is a most serious defamation and this libel deserves, indeed requires, an unreserved apology. He did all in his power to prevent you from causing the accident but was unable to do so and had to sit there fully conscious throughout — a truly terrible experience. In these circumstances for you to write about him in this manner displays an almost unbelievable arrogance.

Your incompetence nearly killed two entirely blameless members of our Team, all of whom had put in years of dedicated work into what was probably the best and most historically important restoration in the World, as you know well having worked on the glazing and bomb-doors for many months yourself.

Your subsequent attempts to blame anything or anyone rather than yourself has 'rubbed salt into the wound' as far as the team is concerned. They were completely devastated and each felt it as deeply as a close personal bereavement. Had you been man enough to apologise and accept responsibility, they may still have had a little respect for you.

Nothing can compensate me for the heartbreak I have suffered with the loss of the Blenheim, for it was at the centre of our lives.

Your comments on this letter are invited — I intend to publish this correspondence unless you can put forward strong reasons why I should not.

Yours truly,

A Blenheim Will Fly Again

Canada 1974

Duxford 1985

Duxford May 1987

Denham June 1987

On 22nd May 1987, a Bristol Blenheim took to the skies for the first time in over forty years to become the sole airworthy example. This first flight followed a meticulous restoration which took twelve years, a small fortune, and some 40,000 man-hours to complete. On 21st June 1987 it was virtually destroyed in an accident at Denham, not due to any mechanical fault, and mercifully with no loss of life.

Despite this devastating blow the British Aerial Museum Team, in response to overwhelming public demand, are ready, willing and able to put a Blenheim back into the air.

They have the experience and expertise, access to the necessary airframe components, the facilities (thanks to the Imperial War Museum at Duxford) *and* the determination and dedication. The Team have demonstrated that they can do it by the superb job they did (virtually unaided) on the first Blenheim rebuild, greatly admired by all who saw it fly during that brief, glorious month. **But they need your help and support to do it again.**

We are honoured that The Master of the Guild of Air Pilots and Air Navigators has kindly agreed to administer the Blenheim Appeal Fund and all donations, large and small, will go directly towards the rebuild. We also need help in kind and can offer commercial sponsorship schemes that will enable you to benefit from the enormous public interest.

The Blenheim was a mainstay of the RAF in the first two desperate years of World War II and the bravery of its crews was unmatched as they fought against heavy odds, often in operations made far more dangerous by the unsuitable tasks they had to perform. No less than 94 Squadrons of the RAF operated Blenheims and they were the only aircraft to serve in every RAF Command and in every Theatre of War.

The British Aerial Museum wish to restore not just the airframe but the proper historic importance of the Blenheim by displaying it at Air Shows in the same way that the RAF Battle of Britain Flight perpetuate the fame of the Spitfire, Hurricane and Lancaster. The Blenheim too, and the extreme courage of its crews, deserves to be commemorated and must not be allowed to fade from the public memory.

Please help us put a Blenheim back in the air once more – the greater your response the sooner the job will be done.

Graham Warner
Founder, British Aerial Museum

The Blenheim Appeal

Building 66, Duxford Airfield, Cambs CB2 4QR.

Please make cheques payable to 'The Blenheim Appeal' – Thank you

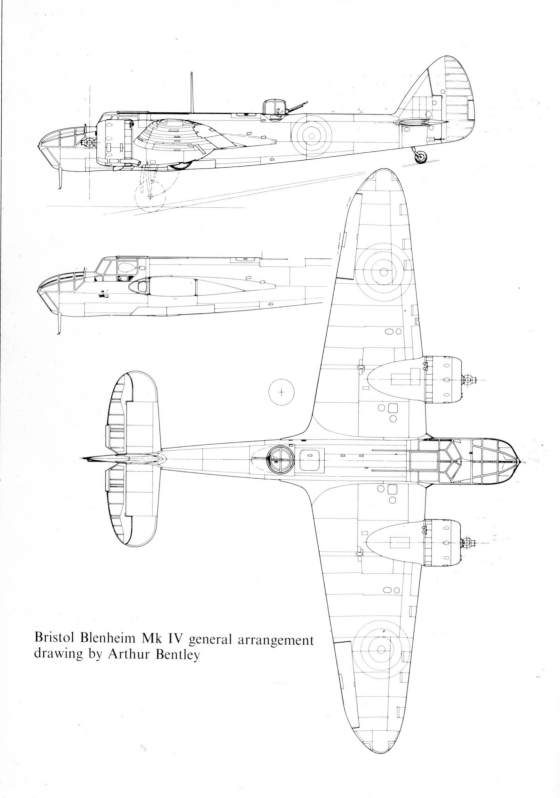

Bristol Blenheim Mk IV general arrangement
drawing by Arthur Bentley